STERLING
Test Prep

MPRE
Unpacked

Rules of
Professional Responsibility
Explained & Applied

3rd edition

3   2   1

ISBN-13: 979-8-8855717-1-5

Sterling Test Prep products are available at quantity discounts.

For more information, contact info@sterling–prep.com

Sterling Test Prep
6 Liberty Square #11
Boston, MA 02109

©2024 Sterling Test Prep
Published by Sterling Test Prep
Printed in the U.S.A.

Customer Satisfaction Guarantee

Your feedback is important because we strive to provide the highest quality prep materials. Email us comments or suggestions.

info@sterling–prep.com

We reply to emails – check your spam folder

Thank you for choosing our book!

STERLING
Test Prep

Thousands of students use our MPRE and bar exam study guides!

Passing the Multistate Professional Responsibility Exam (MPRE) is essential for admission to practice law.

This preparation guide describes the rules of professional responsibility governing the correct answers to MPRE questions. It was developed by legal professionals and law instructors who possess extensive credentials and are admitted to practice law in several jurisdictions. The content is clearly presented and systematically organized for targeted preparation.

By analyzing previously administered tests, the authors identified high-yield items and assembled the rules test-takers must know to answer test questions. Learn these essential ethics rules to make fine-line distinctions among related principles and decide between tough choices on the test. This knowledge is vital to get a passing score on the MPRE.

We look forward to being an essential part of your preparation and wish you immense success in the legal profession!

230714akp

Law Essentials series

Constitutional Law	Criminal Law and Criminal Procedure
Contracts	Business Associations
Evidence	Conflict of Laws
Real Property	Family Law
Torts	Secured Transactions
Civil Procedure	Trusts and Estates

Visit our Amazon store

Bar Exam Preparation Guides

Comprehensive Glossary of Legal Terms

Over 2,100 essential legal terms defined and explained. An excellent reference source for law students, practitioners, and readers seeking an understanding of legal vocabulary and applications.

Visit our Amazon store

Page is intentionally blank

Table of Contents

Table of Contents

Table of Contents

Chapter 2: ATTORNEY-CLIENT RELATIONSHIP (*continued*)

Table of Contents

Table of Contents

Table of Contents

Table of Contents

Table of Contents

Table of Contents

Table of Contents

MPRE Test Information, Preparation

&

Test-Taking Strategies

STERLING
Test Prep

MPRE Test Information

Test overview

The Multistate Professional Responsibility Exam (MPRE) is often the forgotten little sibling of the bar exam.

National Conference of Bar Examiners (NCBE): the MPRE *measures examinees' knowledge and understanding of established standards related to the professional conduct of lawyers.*

MPRE questions are based on the American Bar Association (ABA) *Model Rules of Professional Conduct* and the *ABA Model Code of Judicial Conduct.*

However, the MPRE covers relevant court decisions and procedural and evidentiary rules.

It is crucial to understand the structure, format, and content of the MPRE.

MPRE is required for admission to the bar of all but three U.S. jurisdictions (Wisconsin, Maryland, and Puerto Rico).

Most states administer the MPRE independently of the bar exam. Connecticut and New Jersey accept completing a law-school course on professional responsibility instead of the MPRE.

MPRE is offered three times yearly, typically in March, August, and November.

MPRE is generally taken during the second or third year of law school; most jurisdictions have specific time parameters when the MPRE must be taken, usually referencing the jurisdiction's bar exam.

In some states, applicants must pass the MPRE before taking the bar exam.

MPRE consists of 60 multiple-choice questions (50 *scored* and 10 *unscored questions*) with *two hours* to complete. Each question on the MPRE has *four choices.*

MPRE scores

MPRE is scored on a scale from 50-100 using a process known as equating—taking raw scores and adjusting them for difficulty compared to previous exams.

The average score is usually around 93.

In jurisdictions requiring the MPRE, applicants must obtain a passing MPRE score before admission to the bar.

Each jurisdiction determines the minimum passing score for the MPRE.

Passing scores range from 75-86, with most jurisdictions setting *minimums* at 80 or 85.

California and Utah are known to require the highest passing scores.

Score reporting

MPRE scores are posted to NCBE accounts within weeks and can only be accessed until the next test administration.

Save the score while available or request an MPRE *Unofficial Score Transcript*.

NCBE reports MPRE scores to jurisdictions designated during exam registration.

MPRE Preparation

Preparation challenges

The Multistate Professional Responsibility Exam (MPRE) is a *challenging exam.*

Even though the MPRE is easier than the bar exam, about *one in four test takers fails.*

Nevertheless, like the bar exam, it can be successfully managed with a good plan, study, and practice. It is an exam that should be taken seriously.

Difficulty lies not only in the material but also in the *logistics* of MPRE preparation.

The exam schedule (August, November, and March) presents the first difficulty.

Most students take the MPRE before graduation; they are forced to take the exam either at the beginning or middle of the fall or middle of the spring semester.

Students are busy with classes, extra-curricular activities, internships, and externships.

For students in their third year, there are additional distractors of searching for a job and planning for the bar exam, including submitting their bar application.

Given the tasks students tackle during these times, it can be challenging to find time to study and focus on the MPRE.

Preparation mistakes

Another difficulty presented by the MPRE is the *subject matter* itself.

Fundamentals of legal ethics are relatively *common sense.*

The difficulty with the subject, however, is two-fold.

First, many students have *no significant legal experience* before taking their Professional Responsibility class in law school. This means that the subject matter is *abstract.*

Like the Rules of Civil Procedure to the first semester 1L, the Model Rules of Professional Responsibility *without context* of the complexities of lawyer-client relationships or the general practice of law can be confusing.

Secondly, it is human nature to have a positive, idealized image of themself.

When studying ethics, it is hard for students to internalize the rules as there is a certain sense for the student that *this will never happen to me,* or *I would never do something "unethical.*

This combination can be *challenging to overcome* along with other factors affecting an examinee's performance.

If 3L students taking the exam in August do not pass, there are limited choices to repeat the exam before graduation.

The MPRE is for a few hours on a Saturday morning.

So, given the difficulties and the seemingly unserious space the MPRE inhabits, students often fail to approach the MPRE with the *seriousness necessary to succeed* on the exam.

Students that do not think the exam is serious will be ill-prepared and *risk failing the exam*.

However, students are distracted, and the material is so abstract that it is challenging to have the motivation to approach the MPRE with the depth *necessary for success*.

However, with serious attention and awareness about the MPRE, taking and passing the MPRE can be something each student can manage successfully and pass on the first try.

Scheduling the MPRE

Most schools require, and each school offers, a class on professional responsibility.

Take the ethics class (Professional Responsibility) required by law school before taking the MPRE to maximize the chances of passing the first time.

Some schools focus more on state ethics laws, whereas others focus on the ABA rules.

In either case, enough similarities and overlaps cover the most significant material.

Learn the fundamental principles of ethics law and how judges commonly apply them.

If you are taking a professional responsibility course, the motivation to study the rules and to prepare for the exam is aligned with the MPRE.

Class material and the professor work through the professional responsibility material.

The professor can make abstract principles seem real and communicate scenarios to show how *even well-meaning attorneys* can find themselves in precarious situations.

Study plan

Keys to exam success are less often found in the execution and more often in *the process*.

Building a *simple study plan* before the exam helps ensure you are ready for test day.

A study plan should consist of 5-10 hours a week, focusing on *learning the material* (i.e., rules and exceptions) and *practicing sample questions*.

With any plan, the success of the plan *requires commitment*.

Blocking off study hours each week and adhering to them ensures the *time* and *work necessary* for success in passing the MPRE.

Sample study plan

> ***Week 1:*** (four weeks before MPRE)
>
> Study 2-3 hours Wednesday and 2-3 hours Friday.
>
> Place time and dates on study calendar
>
> Generate study calendar with topics and dates specified.
>
> Focus on learning and memorizing *rules*.
>
> Do *not* start with practice exams.
>
> Learn the law *before* answering questions.
>
> ***Week 2:*** (three weeks before MPRE)
>
> Study 2-3 hours Wednesday and 2-3 hours Friday.
>
> *Review* rules and *introduce practice questions*.
>
> ***Week 3:*** (two weeks before MPRE)
>
> Study 2-3 hours on Saturday and 2-3 hours on Sunday.
>
> Review challenging *topics* and *specific rules* of your *outline*.
>
> Make a *condensed outline* with personalized annotations.
>
> ***Week 4:*** (one week before MPRE on Saturday)
>
> Study 2-3 hours on Tuesday and 2-3 hours on Thursday.
>
> *Review condensed outlines* for reinforced learning of *governing law*.
>
> Focus on *practice exams*.

Study plan considerations

Allow more time *if you*:

- did not take Professional Responsibility in law school
- do not feel comfortable with MPRE material
- are not proficient at standardized tests
- struggle with multiple-choice questions
- score lower than mean on standardized exams

MPRE is "high stakes."

You cannot sit for the bar exam or practice law without passing the MPRE.

Tested topics

Not all areas are treated equally; some are tested more than others.

National Conference of Bar Examiners (NCBE) has a web page with exam details.

In addition to the Model Rules of Professional Responsibility, NCBE reports the scope and coverage of subjects tested on the MPRE.

Spend study time efficiently, *focusing on highly tested topics*.

Allocate study time according to the amount of each subject tested.

Build a *checklist of subjects* and a *study schedule* around these subjects.

For example, *judicial conduct* is only 2-8% of the MPRE.

Questions focused on *attorney-client confidentiality* are 6–12% (3–6 questions).

The most highly tested subject is *conflicts of interest*, comprising 12–18% (6–9 questions).

Keywords and phrases

Law uses *nuanced language*.

Keywords and phrases can make the difference between *passing* or retaking the exam.

Call of the question often uses terminology.

As you study, think about how you might be asked questions and how to integrate keywords and phrases in answers.

Complete and review practice questions to identify keywords and phrases.

Learning these keywords and phrases will allow you to recognize certain aspects being tested and what the examiners are looking for.

For example, *is a lawyer subject to discipline* is different than *is a lawyer subject to civil liability?*"

In disciplinary issues, the client does *not* have to prove duty, breach, cause, and harm.

In civil liability, the client *must* prove duty, breach, cause, and harm. It is often hard to prove that a lawyer's breach of duty caused harm.

Watch for "may" and "must" because they denote mandatory *vs*. permissive.

Identifying these nuances saves time and earns valuable points.

Rules before practice questions

Students make the mistake of simply diving into practice questions when studying for MPRE.

The problem with that approach is that you are applying rules of law not yet known or understood.

Start with subject review materials to learn the rule of law, organized and cohesively.

Focus on rules where clients can give informed consent and waive potential ethical issues.

Practicing questions

Practice as much as possible

Knowing the material is not enough; you *must practice how* you will be examined.

As with the bar exam, one critical aspect of studying for the MPRE is doing *as many practice questions as possible.*

MPRE questions have a *unique* structure, style, phrasing, and rhythm.

An effective way to succeed is to do *countless practice questions.*

Released MPRE questions

MPRE is written and administered by NCBE, and they release *questions for purchase.*

Released questions will be the most like the exam because the NCBE created them.

Released practice questions allow you to discover fact patterns, complexity, length, rules, and structure like the MPRE.

Slow and methodical practice

Timing is *not important* at the beginning of MPRE practice.

Take time to *dissect questions* and understand *what* and *how* it is tested.

Reviewing correct and incorrect answers

Review answered questions to distinguish relevant facts and identify red herrings.

Read the answers and understand questions answered incorrectly and correctly.

Explain why other answer choices were wrong.

Evaluate your understanding and knowledge of the subject.

Compare your rationale to the examiners.

Notes for active learning

MPRE Test-Taking Strategies

Fact patterns

Read and understand the *facts* and the *call of the question.*

Focus on the last sentence of the prompt first (i.e., *call of the question*).

Call of the question identifies what to look for when reading the question stem.

Start at the beginning of the question and read the fact pattern.

Identify critical actors, actions, and circumstances as cues for the ethical issue tested.

Because of exceptions to rules and factors to consider, the correct answer often depends on *one line in the fact pattern.*

Read the fact pattern carefully to avoid missing factors *changing the answer.*

Reading for speed rather than actively noting key elements, traps the student as intended.

Active reading of fact patterns considering the *call of the question* focuses on essential details.

Lawyer's behavior

MPRE is concerned about the *actions of lawyers*, so give special attention to the actions of any lawyer in the fact pattern.

Questions often present fact patterns that *revolve around non-lawyers* (e.g., a paralegal, an accountant, a client) taking a specific action.

Examiners are not testing whether the non-lawyer's actions are unethical, so be sure to look carefully at what the lawyer is doing.

Information that is not relevant to the behavior of an attorney is typically a red herring.

Call of the question

The "*call of the question*" follows the fact pattern and provides the *question asked.*

Call of the question for the MPRE is mainly one of two questions:

> 1) Was the lawyer's (e.g., attorney, judge) conduct *proper*? or

> 2) Is the lawyer (e.g., attorney, judge) *subject to discipline*?

Questions ask, "*Was the lawyer's action right or wrong?*" MPRE questions are predictable.

Be attentive to whether the question is positive (*proper*) or negative (*subject to discipline*).

Active reading of the *call of the question* prevents wasting time re-reading questions.

Rules

After reading *call of the question*, the next step is crucial and requires *memorized rules*.

If you are well-prepared, you actively *read facts* and recognize *rules tested*.

Recall the *rule and its exceptions*.

Instead of recalling a rule, recall a *general principle*.

However, what if you cannot remember the rule or whether an *exception applies*?

Focus on what are the lawyer's actions, and what *ethical dilemma* do they pose?

Based on what you extract from the *call of the question* and *facts*, can you recall a *general principle* that applies to this situation?

For example, lawyers may not deceive, so advertisements with *misinformation are unethical*.

Beware of *exceptions to rules*!

A misleading answer choice may state a general rule of law, which sounds correct.

While the general rule of law may be correct, *check* whether *exceptions* apply to the facts.

Predicting answers

Slow down.

While it may be natural to immediately skim the answer choices after reading a question, the best strategy is to predict the answer *before* looking at the choices.

Predicting the answer uses a concise statement you generate in response to *call of the question* based on the *fact pattern* and *actions of critical participants* (e.g., the lawyer)

Predicting answers *saves time* and prevents being tricked by *shrewdly worded answers*.

Stop and affirm what you think the answer is *before* evaluating the choices.

Recalling rules helps *predict answers*.

Choose the correct answer based on your recollection of *rule* and *predicted answer*.

Mentally explain why the answer is what you *predict*.

Mentally explain why the answer is what you *chose*.

Resolve any discrepancies between your prediction and answer choice; does the needed modification of predicted answer correlate with your analysis?

Eliminating answers

This tip ties back to the emphasis placed on *memorizing rules*.

Better memorization equals a better chance *of identifying wrong answers*.

This simple advice can have hugely beneficial results.

Like the call of the question, answer choices are predictable: there will likely be two "yes" options and two "no" options.

If you cannot predict the answer in its entirety (Yes, because…), you should be able to narrow the answer choices down to the two "yes" or the two "no" answers ("yes, the lawyer is subject to discipline," or "no, the conduct was proper.")

Eliminate choices contradicting the facts in the prompt.

MPRE may include choices that do not align with the facts presented.

Pay attention for unrelated choices as a straightforward way to eliminate incorrect answers.

Read the answer choice in its *entirety before* eliminating it.

Many test-takers have been alerted to a fact pattern mentioned in the answer's reasoning.

If an answer choice mentions a fact that would make an otherwise ethical action unethical (or vice versa), pause and ensure you did not overlook this crucial fact in the fact pattern!

Educated guessing

Avoid "no harm, no foul" answer choices; choices stating that the lawyer's actions should *not* be subject to discipline because *no one got hurt*.

While these answer choices may appear harmless, they are generally wrong.

Typically, incorrect because legal ethics rules operate *irrespective of harm* alleged.

If you cannot recall the rule and resort to guessing, rely on *common sense* since many legal ethics rules are common sense.

Focused preparation

- Rewrite nuanced rules hardest to understand or memorize.

- Express concepts in your own words to *clarify* and *improve retention*.

- Blank answers equal wrong answers so *do not leave* questions unanswered.

- Use flashcards and prepare condensed outlines of persistent issues.

- Have somebody quiz you with preselected materials.

- Review before bed; studies show *studying before sleep* improves retention.

- Listen to audio outlines.

- If anxious, take deep breaths, realize you are not alone and *focus on progress*.

- Eat healthy, exercise, and get enough sleep.

- Follow test-day rules; what you must and cannot bring.

- Prepare everything needed at least one day before the exam.

- *Arrive early* for less stress, and less stress typically means better performance.

- Preparation is a *marathon* and not a sprint – avoid burnout with *balanced lifestyle.*

Chapter 1

Rules of Professional Responsibility

American Bar Association Rules of Professional Conduct

Sources of authority

American Bar Association(ABA) Rules of Professional Conduct address the following.

Responsibilities to clients

As a member of the legal profession, an attorney is:

1) a *representative of clients*,

2) an *officer of the legal system*, and

3) a *public citizen with special responsibilities*.

As a representative of clients, an attorney performs several functions.

As an *advisor*, an attorney provides clients with an informed understanding of their legal rights and obligations and explains their practical implications.

As an *advocate*, an attorney zealously asserts the client's position under the rules of the adversary system.

As a *negotiator*, an attorney seeks an advantage for the client but is consistent with the requirements of honest dealings.

As an *evaluator*, an attorney examines a client's legal affairs and reports them to the client or others.

Lawyers may serve as a third-party neutral, a nonrepresentational role helping parties resolve disputes or other matters.

Rules apply directly to lawyers who serve as third-party neutrals.

Rules apply to lawyers who are not practicing but acting in a nonprofessional capacity.

For example, an attorney who commits fraud in business is subject to discipline for engaging in conduct involving dishonesty, fraud, deceit, or misrepresentation.

A lawyer should be *competent, prompt*, and *diligent* in professional functions.

An attorney should *maintain communication* with a client concerning representation.

An attorney should *keep in confidence* information relating to the representation of a client except as disclosure is *required* or *permitted* by the Rules of Professional Conduct or laws.

Responsibilities to the profession

A lawyer's conduct should conform to the requirements of the law, both in professional service to clients and in the lawyer's business and personal affairs.

Attorney should use law's procedures for legitimate purposes and not harass or intimidate.

A lawyer should demonstrate respect for the legal system and for those who serve it, including judges, other lawyers, and public officials.

Lawyers have a duty to challenge rectitude of official actions, they must uphold legal process.

As a public citizen, a lawyer should seek improvement of the law, access to the legal system, the administration of justice, and the quality of service rendered by the legal profession.

A lawyer should help the legal profession pursue these objectives and aid the bar in regulating itself in the public interest.

As a member of a learned profession, a lawyer should cultivate knowledge of law beyond its use for clients, employ that knowledge in reforming the law, and strengthen legal education.

A lawyer should further the public's understanding of and confidence in the rule of law and the justice system because legal institutions in a constitutional democracy depend on participation to maintain their authority.

Responsibilities to justice

A lawyer should be mindful of deficiencies in the administration of justice and the fact that some people cannot afford legal assistance.

Lawyers should devote professional time and resources and use civic influence to ensure equal access to our justice system for those who cannot afford adequate legal counsel.

A lawyer should strive to attain the highest skill level, improve the legal profession, and exemplify the legal profession's ideals of public service.

Rules of Professional Conduct and substantive and procedural law prescribe many of a lawyer's professional responsibilities.

However, personal conscience and peers also guide a lawyer.

A lawyer's responsibilities as a representative of clients, an officer of the legal system, and a public citizen are usually harmonious.

Thus, when an opposing party is well represented, an attorney can be a zealous advocate on behalf of a client and simultaneously assume that justice is being done.

Preserving client confidence ordinarily serves the public interest because people are more likely to seek legal advice and heed legal obligations knowing communications are private.

Ethical issues

In legal practice, conflicting responsibilities are encountered.

Complex ethical problems arise from conflict between a lawyer's responsibilities to clients, the legal system, and the lawyer's interest in remaining ethical while earning a good living.

The Rules of Professional Conduct often prescribe terms for resolving such conflicts.

However, complex issues of professional discretion arise within the framework of these rules.

Such issues must be resolved by exercising sensitive professional and moral judgment guided by the Rules' fundamental principles.

These principles include the lawyer's obligation to protect and pursue a client's legitimate interests while maintaining a professional, courteous, and civil attitude toward others.

Self-governing profession

The legal profession is self-governing.

Other professions have been granted powers of self-government; however, the legal profession is unique because of the *close relationship* between the profession, government, and law enforcement processes.

This connection is manifested in authority over the legal profession vested in courts.

An independent legal profession is essential in preserving government under the law, for abuse of legal authority is more readily challenged by a profession whose members are not dependent on the government for the right to practice.

Self-regulation maintains the legal profession's independence from government domination.

The legal profession's relative autonomy has special *responsibilities of self-government*.

The profession is responsible for ensuring that its regulations are conceived in the *public interest* and not in furtherance of parochial or self-interested concerns of the bar.

Every lawyer is responsible for observing the *Rules of Professional Conduct*.

A lawyer should encourage professional conduct by all lawyers.

Neglecting rules compromises the independence of the profession and interests it serves.

Lawyers play a vital role in the preservation of society.

This role requires an understanding from lawyers of their relationship to our legal system.

When properly applied, the Rules of Professional Conduct define that relationship.

Rules scope

Rules of Professional Conduct are *rules of reason.*

Rules of Professional Conduct should be interpreted as *legal representation* and *law itself.*

Rules are imperatives when cast in terms *"shall"* or *"shall not."*

Imperatives define proper conduct for the purposes of *professional discipline.*

Rules are permissive and cast in terms "may" and define areas under the Rules where the lawyer has the discretion to *exercise professional judgment.*

No disciplinary action should be taken when the lawyer acts within the *bounds of discretion.*

Rules define the nature of relationships between the attorney and others.

Rules are obligatory, disciplinary, constitutive, and descriptive to *define the lawyer's professional role.*

Rules presuppose a *larger legal context* shaping the lawyer's role.

Context includes *court rules* and *statutes* relating to matters of licensure, laws defining *specific obligations of lawyers*, and *substantive* and *procedural law.*

Rule compliance

Rules provide a framework for the *ethical practice of law.*

Rules do not exhaust moral and ethical considerations, for no worthwhile human activity can be *entirely defined by rules.*

Compliance with the Rules, and laws in society, depends upon:

1) understanding and voluntary *compliance,*

2) peer and public *opinion reinforcement,* and

3) enforcement through *disciplinary proceedings.*

Attorney-client duties

A lawyer's authority and responsibility are defined by *principles of substantive law*.

Principles external to these Rules determine whether an attorney-client relationship exists.

Most duties flow from the *attorney-client relationship* after the client has requested the attorney to *render legal services* and *the lawyer has agreed.*

Legal provisions, including constitutional, statutory, and common law, entrust the responsibilities of government lawyers to *shift authority* for legal matters ordinarily vested in the client for private attorney-client relationships.

For example, a governmental agency attorney may have authority on behalf of the government to *decide upon a settlement* or *whether to appeal an adverse judgment.*

Such authority is vested in the *attorney general*, the state's attorney in state government, and their federal counterparts.

Lawyers under the supervision of officers may be authorized to represent several government agencies in legal controversies, while a *private lawyer cannot represent multiple clients.*

Rules do *not* abrogate any such authority to represent multiple clients.

Rule violations

Failure to comply with an obligation or prohibition imposed by Rules is a basis for invoking the disciplinary process.

Rules presuppose that disciplinary assessment of a lawyer's conduct will be made based on the facts and circumstances as they existed at the time of the conduct and recognition that a lawyer often must act upon uncertain or incomplete evidence of the situation.

Rules presuppose whether discipline should be imposed for a violation, and the severity of a sanction depends on the circumstances, such as the *willfulness* and *seriousness* of the violation, *extenuating factors*, and *previous violations.*

Rules guide lawyers and provide a structure for regulating conduct through *disciplinary agencies*, not the basis for civil liability.

Rule violations should *not* give rise to a cause of action against a lawyer, *nor* should it create any *presumption* in such a case that a *legal duty has been breached.*

Rule violations do *not necessarily* warrant a disciplinary remedy, such as disqualifying a lawyer in pending litigation.

Rules misapplied

Rules' purpose can be subverted when opposing parties use them as *procedural weapons*.

The fact that a Rule is a just basis for a lawyer's self-assessment or for sanctioning a lawyer under the administration of a disciplinary authority does *not imply* that an antagonist in a collateral proceeding or transaction has *standing to seek enforcement* of Rules.

Since the Rules establish standards of conduct by lawyers, a lawyer's violation of a Rule may be evidence of a breach of the *applicable standard of conduct*.

Terminology Rule 1.0

Definitions

Attorney (or *lawyer*) – a person who graduated from law school, passed the bar exam in the state where they practice law and is a member of the State Bar Association in the state where they practice. *An attorney acts as a practitioner in a court of law. The terms attorney and lawyer are interchangeable for the following context.*

Belief – the person involved supposed the fact in question to be true. A person's belief may be inferred from circumstances.

Confirmed in writing – informed consent of a person denotes informed consent given in writing by the person or a writing that a lawyer promptly transmits to the person confirming an oral informed consent. If obtaining or transmitting the writing when the person gives informed consent is not feasible, then the lawyer must obtain or transmit it within a reasonable time.

Firm (or *law firm*) – lawyers in a law partnership, professional corporation, sole proprietorship, or other association authorized to practice law; or lawyers employed in a legal services organization or the legal department of a corporation or other organization.

Fraud (or *fraudulent*) – conduct that is deceptive and dishonest under the substantive or procedural law of the applicable jurisdiction and has a purpose of deceiving.

Informed consent – an agreement by a person to a proposed course of conduct after the lawyer has communicated adequate information and explanation about the material risks of and reasonably available alternatives to the proposed course of conduct.

Knowingly (*known* or *knows*) – actual knowledge of the fact in question. A person's knowledge may be inferred from circumstances.

Lawyer (or *attorney*) – someone who has completed law school, obtained a JD degree and has not yet passed the Bar exam. *The terms attorney and lawyer are interchangeable for the following context.*

Material – an essential matter of clear and weighty importance about degree or extent.

Partner – a member of a partnership, a shareholder in a law firm organized as a professional corporation, or a member of an association authorized to practice law.

Reasonable (or *reasonably*) – conduct by a lawyer denotes the conduct of a sensible, prudent, and competent lawyer.

Reasonable belief (or *reasonably believes*) – lawyer believes the matter in question and that the circumstances are such that the belief is fair and sensible.

Reasonably – sensible prudence and competence to ascertain the matter in question.

Screened – the isolation of a lawyer from participation in a matter through the timely imposition of procedures within a firm that is adequate to protect information that the isolated lawyer is obligated to protect under these Rules or other laws.

Signed writing – includes an electronic sound, symbol, or process attached to or logically associated with a writing and executed or adopted by a person intending to sign the writing.

Substantial – a material matter of clear and weighty importance about degree or extent.

Tribunal – a court, an arbitrator in a binding arbitration proceeding, or a legislative body, administrative agency, or other body acting in an adjudicative capacity. A legislative body, administrative agency, or other body acts in an adjudicative capacity when a neutral official, after presenting evidence or legal argument by a party or parties, renders a binding legal judgment directly affecting a party's interests in a particular matter.

Writing (or *written*) – a tangible or electronic record of a communication or representation, including handwriting, typewriting, printing, photography, audio or video recording, and electronic communications.

Chapter 2

Attorney–Client Relationship

Implied-In-Law Incidents of the Attorney-Client Relationship

Competence [Rule 1.1]

Rule 1.1 requires that a lawyer either provide competent representation to a client or decline the representation if they cannot do so.

Legal knowledge and skill

A lawyer may obtain the *required legal knowledge* and *skill* by *studying or associating* with a lawyer established as competent in the field.

A more *lenient standard of competence* applies when a lawyer is required in an *emergency*.

Adequate preparation

To meet the required competence standard, a lawyer must *adequately prepare* to represent the client in the matter they have been engaged in.

Relationship scope [Rule 1.2]

Client is the *principal*, and the attorney is the *agent* in the attorney-client relationship.

Client has the ultimate authority to determine the *purposes* to be served by the representation.

In consultation with the client, the attorney ordinarily has the right to determine *how* the *objectives* of the relationship will be pursued [Rule 1.2(a)].

Since the relationship is *contractual,* the attorney, in consultation with client and with client's consent, can *limit the scope of representation* [Rule 1.2(c)].

Lawyer does *not* violate this Rule by acceding to *reasonable requests* of opposing counsel, which do *not* prejudice their client's rights, being *punctual in fulfilling professional commitments*, *avoiding offensive tactics*, or treating with *courtesy and consideration* all persons involved in the legal process.

Client's decisions [Rule 1.2]

Decisions specifically allocated to the client.

Rule 1.2(a) explicitly allocates the following *decisions to the client*:

1) to accept an *offer of settlement* in a civil case or *plea bargain* in a criminal case;

2) the *plea* to be entered;

3) whether to *waive jury trial*; and

4) whether the *client will testify*.

Limitations regarding fraud and criminal conduct

If the client requests or demands that the attorney engages in fraud or criminal conduct during their relationship, the attorney must not do so but may discuss appropriate means to achieve the client's objectives [Rule 1(d)].

Lawyer must *withdraw from representation* if the client insists the attorney engages in *fraudulent or illegal conduct* [Rule 1.16].

Exception permits an attorney to participate in an *activity violating the law to test it.*

Client under disability

If the client cannot legally make decisions because of mental incapacity, the disabled person's *legal guardian*, if one exists, makes the decisions for the client.

If there are *no legal guardians*, the *lawyer can function as the substitute legal guardian* and make *decisions ordinarily reserved for the client.*

Diligence [Rule 1.3]

Lawyer shall act with *reasonable diligence* and *promptness* in representing a client.

Lawyer should represent a client *zealously within the bounds of the law.*

Lawyer must complete work on the client's matter *promptly and conclude it* unless they have been terminated before the matter is completed.

To represent a client zealously, the lawyer may take *legal and ethical measures* necessary to *promote their client's interest.*

Communications [Rule 1.4]

Necessary information

Attorney has an *affirmative and enforceable duty* to keep a client *reasonably informed* about the status of the matter and *promptly comply with reasonable requests for information.*

Attorney must explain a matter to the extent reasonably necessary to permit the *client to make informed decisions* regarding the representation [Rule 1.4(b)].

Adequacy of communication

An attorney must communicate information to the client "*appropriate for a client who is a comprehending and responsible adult.*"

A different level of communication is required when the client is a *minor* or has a *mental disability*. Routine matters can be communicated with *less frequency.*

Emergencies

"Practical exigency" may require a lawyer to act for a client *without consultation*.

Withholding information

In some instances, a lawyer may be justified in *delaying the transmission* of information when the client would likely react *imprudently* to an immediate communication.

Lawyers may not transmit information to their clients if they are forbidden by a *court ruling*, such as a *discovery order* that permits a lawyer to inspect documents but *forbids* them to disclose the inspection results to their client.

Notes for active learning

Fees [Rule 1.5]

Reasonable fees

Attorney has an affirmative obligation to charge a *reasonable fee*.

If the client has agreed to the *unreasonable fee*, the lawyer may *not enforce* the agreement for the unreasonable amount.

A lawyer is subject to *discipline for charging* an unreasonable fee [Rule 1.5].

Rules contain a *nonexclusive list* of eight factors to determine if a *fee is reasonable*.

1) time and labor required, the novelty and difficulty of the questions involved, and the skill requisite to perform the legal services properly;

2) likelihood, if apparent to the client, that the acceptance of one particular employment will preclude other employment by the lawyer;

3) fee customarily charged in the locality for similar legal services;

4) amount involved and the results obtained;

5) time limitation imposed by the client or by circumstances;

6) nature and length of the professional relationship with client;

7) experience, reputation, and ability of the lawyer performing services; and

8) whether fee is fixed or contingent.

Fee agreements and retainers

When a lawyer has not regularly represented a client, the basis or rate of the fee shall be:

communicated to the client,

preferably in writing,

before or within a *reasonable time* after the commencement of representation.

Attorney may collect a fee in *advance as a retainer* but must *return any unearned portion*.

Non-refundable retainer is permitted if they forgo legal work to undertake representation.

Collecting fees

Credit permitted

Attorney may use *credit cards* to collect fees.

Attorney may arrange a *bank loan* for their client.

Attorney may obtain a lien upon a potential recovery to ensure the fee is paid.

Payment in the form of property

If the property is not a prohibited interest in litigation, a lawyer may receive a transfer of property by the client as a fee.

Attorney cannot take advantage of client if attorney has *superior property value knowledge*.

Disputes over fees

Lawyer may file a suit to collect fees, but only *after* trying to resolve the matter without suit.

Attorney should first use established *arbitration* or *mediation services*, such as the procedure established by the State Bar Association to resolve fee disputes.

Contingent fees

Under a contingent fee agreement, a client must pay a fee *only if* there is a favorable outcome; the lawyer *can agree* to be responsible for *litigation expenses* if there is no recovery.

Except when prohibited, as discussed below, *contingent fees are valid*.

Prohibited contingent fees

Contingent fees are prohibited when representing a defendant in a *criminal case* [Rule 1.5(d)].

Contingent fees are *prohibited* in domestic relations; payment or amount contingent upon securing a divorce, the amount of alimony or support, or property settlement [Rule 1.5(d)].

Requirements of a valid contingent fee agreement

Contingent fee agreements shall be in *writing*.

Contingent fee agreements must state the:

> name and address of each client and lawyer retained,
>
> nature of the claim or controversy,
>
> method by which the contingent fee will be determined, and
>
> whether the percentages is calculated before or after expenses are deducted.

Contingent fee agreements must state *percentages* accrued to the lawyer if the case is *settled*, *tried*, and *tried and appealed*.

Contingent fee agreements must be *delivered to the client*, and the lawyer must retain a copy and *proof of delivery*.

Writing required after the matter

When the contingent fee matter concludes, the attorney must describe the *outcome* of the case to the client in *writing*.

Attorney must furnish the client with an *accounting* for a recovery showing the:

1) total *amount recovered*,

2) *method of calculating* the contingent fee,

3) *deductions for expenses*, and

4) *amount remitted* to the client.

Division of legal fees [Rule 1.5(e)]

Division of fees is when two lawyers, not from the same firm, remit a *single bill* to the client.

Division of fees between members of the *same firm* is permitted and *not* subject to this Rule.

Valid *fee divisions*:

1) must be *proportional to work performed* by each lawyer, or each lawyer must agree, by a written agreement *with* the client, to be *jointly responsible* for the total representation,

2) client must *consent* to the division, including the *share* each lawyer receives, and the agreement is confirmed in *writing*; and,

3) total fee charged to the client must be *reasonable* (i.e., *not more* than without the division).

Professional responsibility vignette 1

Cheryl experienced an infection at the surgical incision's point following a routine appendectomy. She mentioned this to her friend, Steve, a corporate lawyer who referred her to Lynne, his sister-in-law, who specialized in medical malpractice claims.

Cheryl retained Lynne to sue Robert, the surgeon who had performed the appendectomy, for negligence. In a telephone conversation, Lynne told Cheryl that her fee would be about one-third of any recovery.

Lynne asked, and Cheryl sent her a check for $5,000 "to cover expert and other expenses," Lynne used the money to pay the due account of an expert she retained in an unrelated case.

Cheryl admitted confidentially to Lynne that she lied at her deposition concerning the extent of her physical and emotional injuries. Based chiefly on that testimony, Robert offered to settle the case for $100,000, an amount far beyond Lynne's estimate of the value of the claim. Cheryl accepted the offer.

Robert delivered a check in that amount to Lynne payable to "Lynne, as the attorney for Cheryl." Lynne endorsed and deposited the check in her firm's operating account but did not inform Cheryl of its receipt.

Several months later, Cheryl asked Lynne about the status of the case. Lynne said she would investigate it and then wrote a check to Cheryl for $65,000, retaining $35,000 for herself, which she divided, unknown to Cheryl, with Steve, the referring lawyer. After receiving the check, Cheryl demanded that Lynne send her the settlement balance and an accounting of the $5,000 advance by Cheryl. Lynne refused, and Cheryl complained about Lynne's actions.

Please prepare a memorandum concerning the merits of the complaint.

Outline of facts

        Contingent Fee Agreement – Rule 1.5 must be in writing

        Violation of rule with respect to client funds

        Misrepresentation to another lawyer for failure to correct lies in deposition

        Mishandling of settlement

        Placed it in the wrong account

        Failed to pay promptly

        Failed to pay 2/3 due to Cheryl

        Failed to account for an advance on expenses

        Payment of referral fee to Steve

Contingent fee agreement: a contingent fee agreement *shall be in writing*.

It must state the *name and address* of each client and lawyers to be retained, nature of the claim or controversy, method by which contingent fee will be determined, and whether the percentages will be calculated before or after expenses are deducted [Rule 1.5].

Contingent fee agreement must also state the percentage or percentages which will accrue to the lawyer if the case is settled if it is tried, and if it is tried and appealed.

A copy of the agreement must be delivered to the client, and the lawyer must retain a copy of the agreement and proof of its delivery to the client.

Lynne failed to comply with the requirements of a contingent fee agreement because there was no written agreement.

The agreement failed to specify if the contingency was calculated before or after expenses and did not specify the percentages to be applied if the case was *settled, tried,* or *appealed.*

Trust account: money given to a lawyer in advance for expenses must be placed in the client's funds account and only be used for purposes for which it was advanced [Rule 1.15].

Lynne was required to place advanced funds to pay litigation expenses in her clients' funds account and to use those funds only for those expenses. She did not place the money in a client's fund account and used it *improperly to pay unrelated* expert expenses.

When the contingent fee matter is concluded, the attorney must describe the outcome of the case to the client *in writing*.

Lawyer must furnish the client with an accounting when there has been a recovery showing the *total amount recovered, method of calculating* the contingent fee, *deductions of expenses,* and *amount remitted* to the client [Rule 1.15].

Lawyer must *promptly notify* the client or the third person when receiving property belonging to others. Unless permitted by the Rules or by agreement, the lawyer must *promptly deliver* the property to the person entitled to receive it [Rule 1.15].

When a lawyer receives *money,* such as a settlement check, which belongs to the lawyer and the client jointly, the *entire amount* must be placed in the *client's funds account*.

If there is *no dispute* on the division of the funds, the lawyer must pay the client the amount due and transfer their portion of the funds to their account [Rule 1.15].

If there is a dispute concerning the division of funds, the client and the lawyer can be paid the amounts undisputedly due each from the client's funds account. However, the disputed amount must remain in the client's funds account until resolved [Rule 1.15].

Mishandling of settlement: Lynne was obliged to deposit the settlement check in her clients' funds account, not her firm's operating account.

She was obligated to promptly inform Lynne that she had received the funds and provide her with an accounting of the funds due her. She did neither [Rule 1.15].

Even if the contingent fee of one-third is deemed reasonable, a doubtful proposition, she owed Cheryl more than she sent her ($66,666.66, not $65,000) and an *accounting for funds* Cheryl advanced for expenses [Rule 1.5].

Referral fees: a division of fees is when two lawyers, not of the same firm, send a single bill to the client.

Fee division between members of the same firm is permitted and is *not* subject to Rule 1.5.

Fee divisions require:

      1)   *total fee* charged must be reasonable (i.e., not more than if without the division);

      2)   *client consent* to the division.

While Lynne could properly pay Steve a referral fee under the Rules of Professional Conduct even though he did not perform legal services on her case, the payment was improper because Cheryl did *not consent* to the *division* of the legal fees.

Confidentiality [Rule 1.6]

Confidentiality required

Lawyer shall not reveal confidential information relative to client representation unless client consents after consultation, except for disclosure *impliedly authorized* to conduct representation, except as provided in other rules [Rule 1.6(a)].

Protected information: scope

Obligation of confidentiality, subject to exceptions, applies to confidential information relating to the representation from all sources.

Confidentiality includes communications covered by attorney-client privilege.

It includes information obtained by the lawyer or their assistants in the representation from public and private sources.

Confidential information obtained by the lawyer before the attorney-client relationship was established, which relates to the case, is *protected if* it relates to the representation.

Protected information: obligations

Unless disclosure comes within an exception, Rule 1.6 prevents a lawyer from disclosing confidential information to anyone except lawyers in the firm and to staff working for the firm who are bound by the disclosure rules.

Lawyer cannot disclose information to an authorized recipient when the lawyer knows that the person receiving the information is likely to disclose it unauthorizedly.

Obligation of *non-disclosure* exists *after* the attorney-client relationship ends.

If the client or former client has *died*, the obligation still exists but can be *waived* by the deceased client's *executor* or *administrator*.

Attorney *cannot* use or reveal protected confidential information to the *disadvantage* of a former client.

Former client's *permission to disclose* confidential information is required before a lawyer can use that information to benefit a new client.

Protected information: disclosure exceptions

Consent

Client *can waive* the protection of this Rule and *consent* to disclosure after consultation.

Implied authority to represent a client

Lawyer can *use and disclose* protected information to *represent the client*.

Lawyer may disclose information to collaborators unless client *explicitly restricts disclosure*.

Lawyer can reveal information to opposing counsel *except for* privileged information that qualifies as *attorney's work product*, sought during discovery, or must be disclosed in other court proceedings.

Lawyer's conduct during representation is in issue

Rule 1.6(b)(5) permits disclosure when the attorney's conduct is at issue:

1) the extent the lawyer believes *necessary to establish a claim* or *defense* on behalf of the lawyer in a controversy with the client.

2) establish a *defense* to a criminal charge or civil claim against the lawyer based upon conduct in which the client was involved.

3) respond to *allegations* in any proceeding concerning the lawyer's representation of the client.

Permissive disclosure

Lawyer is permitted to reveal confidential information when a lawyer reasonably believes that a client will commit a criminal act likely to *result in death or substantial bodily harm*; lawyer has the *right, but not obligation*, to reveal such information as necessary to prevent the act [Rule 1.6(b)(1)].

Lawyer is permitted to use protected information to *prevent* a future *crime* or substantial injury to *commercial interests* and *property* of another [Rule 1.6(b)(2)].

Exception does *not* include *past crimes* committed without lawyer's assistance or complicity.

Litigation matters

Disclosure is required except where a lawyer represents a criminal defendant.

Lawyer must disclose to a tribunal a material fact where disclosure is necessary to avoid assisting a client in committing a criminal or fraudulent act [Rule 3.3(a)(2)].

Lawyer is forbidden from offering evidence that the lawyer knows is false [Rule 3.3(a)(1)].

For example, if a lawyer offers evidence and later knows its falsity, the lawyer shall take appropriate *remedial measures*, including disclosing information protected under Rule 1.6.

Obligations to *inform the tribunal* continue *only until* the *conclusion* of the proceedings.

Perjury by criminal defendant

The difference between a criminal defendant and other clients is that the criminal defendant has a *constitutional right to testify* in their defense and the right to the *assistance of counsel*.

That right does *not* include the right to the *assistance* of a lawyer in committing *perjury*.

Thus, criminal defendants do *not* appear to have greater rights than civil litigants.

Rules do *not* mandate disclosure in the case of a *lying criminal defendant*.

Court order or law

Except for matters protected by *attorney-client privilege*, a lawyer may reveal confidential information required *by law* or *court order* [Rule 1.6(b)(6)].

Attorney-client privilege

Client, as the *holder of the privilege*, has a right to refuse to disclose and prevent others from disclosing confidential communications to facilitate the rendition of professional legal services to the client if the communication is between the lawyer and the client or designated representative.

Attorney-client privilege is *narrower* than protected information under Rule 1.6.

When the legal process requires the lawyer to testify, that attorney's ethical duty is to comply with the *process and reveal* protected information *unless* the information requested is protected by the *attorney-client privilege* or rules protecting the *lawyer's work product*.

Then, the lawyer must assert the privilege and refuse to disclose the protected information.

Exceptions to the attorney-client privilege parallel some exceptions in Rule 1.6.

Attorney-client privilege is *inapplicable* when the purpose of the communication is to further *a crime or commit fraud* or where the issue is a *breach of duty by the lawyer to the client*.

Professional responsibility vignette 2

While George was reviewing a client's confidential documents, he learned that this client was about to sell a new type of baby shampoo that would cause a baby's eyes to sting even though the shampoo bottle's label claimed that a baby's eyes would not be irritated by the shampoo. George has asked whether he may disclose this information to a consumer affairs reporter at a local paper.

Confidential information: a lawyer shall not reveal confidential information related to the representation of a client unless the client consents after consultation [Rule 1.6].

The information about the baby shampoo is confidential and does *not* constitute fraud in which the lawyer's services have been used, a circumstance that would permit disclosure.

George may *not disclose* information obtained to the consumer reporter for a local newspaper.

Loyalty to Clients [Rule 1.7]

Conflicts of interest

Attorney is prohibited from representing client if representation might be *materially limited* because of the lawyer's interests [Rule 1.7(a)].

Interests in conflict with clients

Two types of conflicts between clients:

Direct conflicts are prohibited when a lawyer represents a client where that representation is directly adverse to another client [Rule 1.71(a)(1)].

> Such representation is permitted only if the lawyer reasonably believes the representation will not adversely affect the relationship with the other client *and* each consent after consultation.

Potential conflicts arise when lawyer's responsibilities might materially limit representation to another client [1.7(a)(2)].

> Representation is permitted if the lawyer believes that their representation of the client (as opposed to a relationship with the other client in the case of direct conflict) will *not be adversely affected,* and *each client consents* after consultation.

Declining representation

The lawyer's professional judgment should be exercised within the bounds of the law; for the benefit of the client and free of compromising influences; the lawyer's *loyalty to a client* should not be compromised.

> Attorney should *decline* rendering services if they *know of conflict before* commencing representation.

> Attorney should *withdraw* if the conflict arises *after* representation has commenced and cannot be waived.

Notes for active learning

Third-Party Conflicts with Client [Rule 1.8]

Lawyer and client conflicts

Business transactions with the client

A lawyer is prohibited from entering into a business transaction with a client and from knowingly acquiring ownership, possessory, security, or other pecuniary *interest adverse* to the client unless [Rule 1.8(a)]:

1) transaction and terms on which the lawyer acquires the interest are fair and reasonable; terms of the arrangement are fully disclosed to the client in writing in a form that the client can reasonably understand;

2) client is given a reasonable opportunity to *seek advice* of outside counsel on the transaction; and

3) client *consents in writing*.

Rule applies when *attorney-client relationship* exists between *lawyer* and *business associates*.

Rule is *inapplicable if no* attorney-client relationship exists, and the lawyer is *not* performing legal services because the entity has *independent outside counsel*.

Rule does *not* apply to standard commercial transactions for products and services that client markets to others.

Use of information

Lawyer *cannot use confidential information* relating to the representation of a client to the disadvantage of the client, the lawyer's advantage, or the advantage of a third person unless the *client consents* or Rule 1.6 for confidentiality or Rule 3.3 for the lawyer's responsibilities to the *tribunal requires* such disclosure [Rule 1.8(b)].

Gifts and bequests

Attorney *shall not* prepare an instrument giving the lawyer or person related to the lawyer as a parent, child, sibling, or spouse any substantial gift from a client, including a testamentary gift, except where the *client is related* to the donor [Rule 1.8(c)].

Attorney *cannot* avoid this rule by obtaining the client's consent.

Media rights

Before concluding client representation, a lawyer *shall not* make or negotiate an agreement giving the lawyer the *literary or media rights* to a portrayal or account based in substantial part on information relating to *representation* [Rule 1.8(d)].

Client *consent will not* permit lawyer to negotiate a *literary or media rights* contract, even if granting media rights might be the only way for client to hire exceptionally qualified counsel.

Since the lawyer is *prohibited* from negotiating for media rights, mentioning an expectation of subsequently acquiring them violates this Rule.

Financial assistance to clients

Lawyer shall not provide *financial assistance* to a client in connection with pending or contemplated litigation, except that the lawyer may advance *court costs and expenses of litigation*, repayment *contingent on the outcome* of litigation [Rule 1.8(e)].

Client consent will *not* absolve the lawyer of that *prohibition*.

Attorney representing an indigent client may pay court costs and litigation expenses on the client's behalf.

Malpractice – prospective limitation of liability

Lawyer *shall not* make an agreement limiting the lawyer's liability to a client for malpractice unless permitted by law and the client is independently represented in making the agreement [Rule 1.8(h)(1)].

Malpractice – settling malpractice claims

Lawyer cannot settle an existing malpractice claim with an unrepresented client or former client without first advising the person in writing that independent representation is appropriate [Rule 1.8(h)(2)].

Acquiring an interest in litigation

Attorney is prohibited from acquiring a *proprietary interest* in the *cause of action* or *subject matter of litigation*, *except* that the lawyer may:

1) *acquire a lien* granted by law to secure the lawyer's fee or expenses, and

2) *contract* for a reasonable contingent fee in a civil case [Rule 1.8(i)].

While lawyers are associated in a firm, prohibitions from Rule 1.8 apply to all.

Third parties and client conflicts

Payment by third party to represent client

Attorney is prohibited from *accepting compensation for representing a client* from one other than the client *unless client consents* after consultation and there is *no interference* with the lawyer's independence of *professional judgment* or *lawyer-client relationship.*

Information relating to *representation is confidential*, as required by Rule 1.6 [Rule 1.8(f)].

Direct conflicts – civil cases

Direct conflicts occur most frequently in an *adversarial context* where a lawyer or their firm is on *both sides of one case*. It is *almost impossible to obtain permission to continue*, and the lawyer will often *not represent either party.*

Direct conflict is when a lawyer *represents a client* in one case and *sues that client* in another.

Ordinarily, such a conflict will result in the *lawyer not participating in the second case.*

However, it is possible in large organizations where the cases are unrelated for lawyers to obtain the necessary permission to continue in both cases.

Direct conflicts – criminal cases

Direct conflict exists when representing two defendants jointly accused of the same crime.

Criminal defendant has the *constitutional right* to assistance by counsel.

Lawyer is *rarely permitted* to represent simultaneously *two defendants accused of committing the same crime* because the *possibility of conflict is too great.*

If dual representation is undertaken, an attorney is prohibited from making an aggregated agreement as to *guilty* or *nolo contendere* pleas unless *each client consents after consultation,* including disclosure of the *existence and nature of claims or pleas* involved and the *participation of each in the settlement* [Rule 1.8(g)].

Professional responsibility vignette 3

Frank has been representing Dave, a criminal defendant convicted of income tax evasion. As Dave does not have the money to pay for the appeal of this conviction, Frank has asked whether he may sign a contract with Dave providing that your law firm's compensation for Frank's legal work on Dave's appeal would be an assignment by Dave of all his literary and media rights to a portrayal of Dave's life, criminal trial, and appeal.

Media rights: prior to the conclusion of the representation of a client, a lawyer shall not make or negotiate an agreement giving the lawyer literary or media rights to a portrayal or account based in substantial part on information relating to the representation [Rule 1.8(d)].

Dave may not enter into the agreement. Here, a substantial part of the literary rights, which Frank seeks, is a portrayal of Dave's criminal trial and appeal.

Duties to Former Clients [Rule 1.9]

Direct conflicts with former clients

An attorney may not represent another person in the same or substantially related matter in which that person's interests are materially adverse to the former client's interests unless the former client consents after representation.

If such representation is undertaken, the lawyer cannot use or reveal confidential information obtained in the former relationship in violation of confidentiality obligations under Rule 1.6.

Potential conflicts – litigation representation of multiple parties

Potential conflict exists when a lawyer represents *multiple parties* in tort or other litigation.

When the representation of multiple clients in a single matter is undertaken, the consultation with the potential clients shall include an explanation of the implications of the common representations and the advantages and risks involved [Rule 1.7(a)(2)].

An attorney who represents two or more clients shall *not participate* in making an aggregate settlement of claims or against clients unless each client consents after consultation, including disclosure of the existence and nature of claims and the participation of each party in the settlement [Rule 1.8(g)].

Potential conflicts – insured and insurer

When a defendant is covered by liability insurance and is defended by the insurance company, a potential conflict exists if there is a possibility that the insured might not be covered for the *entire claim* or that the *liability policy does not cover claims* based on specific theories.

The insured must be notified of the *conflict and advised to retain independent counsel.*

Potential conflicts – non-litigation context

In the role of counselor for multiple parties, lawyer frequently encounters potential *conflicts of interest* and must obtain *consent to represent* the multiple parties.

Before asking for consent, the lawyer must believe that:

1) matters of the representation can be resolved on terms compatible with the best interests of all clients;

2) each client be adequately informed to be able to make decisions on the matter;

3) there is negligible risk of material prejudice if the joint representation fails; and

4) common representation can be undertaken impartially without improperly affecting the lawyer's responsibilities to any client.

Dispensation from conflict rules

Both clients must consent before a lawyer can represent a client when a *conflict exists* or when there is a *conflict between clients.*

The attorney seeking a client's consent must satisfy both a *subjective* and *objective test.*

Before a lawyer can seek consent to represent a client when there is a conflict of interest, they must *first subjectively believe* that they can accept the representation even though the lawyer may be limited in exercising *specific options* because of the conflict.

Representation must be *objectively reasonable* under the circumstances.

Lawyer *cannot ask* for consent if a *disinterested lawyer concludes* that a client should not agree to the representation under the circumstances.

Lawyer must *consult with client* concerning the *conflict of interest.*

Consultation with clients about conflict of interest requires the communication of information sufficient to permit the client to realize the *significance of the matter* in question.

Imputed Conflicts of Interest [Rule 1.10]

Imputed disqualifications

In applying Rules 1.7 and 1.8 to determine conflict of interest, the Rules impute the interests of defined groups of additional lawyers to the lawyer whose conflict is in issue and treat all conflicts of the imputed lawyer in making the determination.

Related lawyers

An attorney related to another lawyer as a parent, child, sibling, or spouse shall not represent a client in a representation directly adverse to a person whom the lawyer knows is represented by the other lawyer except upon consent by the client after consultation concerning the relationship [Rule 1.8(i)].

Consent of the client or relative is not required for a lawyer to take on this representation.

Imputed conflict rule only affects a *lawyer individually*, not members of their firm.

Firm members

When lawyers are associated in a firm, none of them shall knowingly represent a client when any of them practicing alone would be prohibited from doing so by Rules 1.7, 1.8(c), or Rule 1.9 [Rule 1.10].

Term "firm" includes lawyers practicing in a private partnership, a professional corporation, a legal department of a corporation, and a legal services organization.

Changing firms

The mechanics of implying the *imputation rules* are different when a lawyer *changes firms*.

Procedures must be set up so that the attorney *cannot disclose* information to their new firm and takes no part in representing clients at the new firm who have a conflict with prior clients.

Affected clients are *informed* of the procedures.

The issue of the ability of a firm from which a lawyer has departed to represent clients adverse to the interests of the client who has left the firm with the departing lawyer is addressed by Rule 1.10(b), which provides that the old firm can represent the clients adverse to those taken by a departing lawyer if no lawyers remain who have information which is material to the representation and is protected by Rules 1.6 and 1.9.

Notes for active learning

Prior Employment [Rule 1.11]

Government service followed by private employment

Lawyer is only prohibited from representing a private client after government service when the lawyer has personally and substantially participated in the matter as a public officer or employee unless the appropriate government agency gives its *informed consent*, confirmed in writing, to the representation. [Rule 1.11(a)].

Personal involvement does not include general supervisory authority over the matter.

The term *"matter"* does *not include* making *policy* or drafting *general regulations*.

Matter is defined under Rule 1.11(e) to include judicial or other proceedings, requests for rulings, contracts, claim controversies, investigations, charges, accusations, arrests, matters involving a specific party, or anything defined as a "matter" by rules of a government agency.

Rule 1.11(a) establishes a more *lenient standard* for lawyers *possessing protected information* when leaving government service and *permits* a former government lawyer to join a firm with *clients with direct conflicts* with the government agency about which the *attorney possesses protected information.*

The only restrictions are that the attorney must be effectively screened from *any participation* in the matter, they *cannot be apportioned* any part of the fee, and *written notice* must be promptly given to the appropriate government agency to enable them to ascertain compliance with the Rule.

Lawyer leaving government service cannot use confidential government information about a *person* they obtained while in government service for the benefit of a client against that person whose information they possess, *even though* the attorney has never had an attorney-client relationship with that person.

Confidential government information is information obtained by governmental authority.

Government information cannot be disclosed if privileged and not available to the public.

Same restrictions are imposed on *government employees* who serve as *judges, adjudicative officers*, and *arbitrators* [Rule 1.12(a)].

Same restrictions are imposed for *imputed disqualification on a judge, adjudicative officers,* or *arbitrator* who leaves a position to join a private firm [Rule 1.12(c)].

Private employment followed by government service

Governmental lawyer is prohibited from participating in matters in which the lawyer participated *personally* and *substantially* while in private practice [Rule 1.11(c)].

However, if the lawyer in public service is the *only person* authorized to act on the matter under *applicable law*, the lawyer *may do so*.

Soliciting employment while in government service

Lawyer in government service, including judges, adjudicative officers, or neutral arbitrators, cannot *negotiate for private employment* while personally and substantially involved in a matter *with either* the opposing party or that party's attorney [Rule 1.11(c)(2)].

Once the matter is *concluded,* a lawyer is *not precluded* from such negotiation.

However, law clerks of judges are permitted to negotiate for employment with law firms having matters on which they participate personally and substantially, but *only after* the law clerk has *notified the judge* presiding over such negotiations.

Former Judge or Other Third-Party Neutral [Rule 1.12]

Prohibited representation

A lawyer shall not represent anyone in connection with a matter in which they participated personally and substantially as a judge or other adjudicative officer or law clerk or as an arbitrator, mediator, or third-party neutral unless all parties to the proceeding give informed consent, confirmed in writing [Rule 1.12(a)].

Employment restrictions

Lawyer shall not negotiate for employment with any person involved as a party or lawyer for a party in which the lawyer participates personally and substantially as a judge or other adjudicative officer or as an arbitrator, mediator, or other third-party neutral.

Lawyer serving as a law clerk may negotiate for employment with a party or lawyer involved in a matter in which the clerk participates personally and substantially, but only after the lawyer has notified the judge or other adjudicative officer.

Disqualified lawyer in a firm

No lawyer in a firm with which that disqualified lawyer is associated may knowingly undertake or continue representation in the matter unless:

> 1) the disqualified lawyer is *timely screened* from any participation in the matter and is *apportioned no part of the fee*; and

> 2) *written notice* is promptly given to the parties and appropriate tribunal.

Private arbitrator selected for an arbitration panel is not prohibited from subsequently representing that party.

Notes for active learning

Organizational Client [Rule 1.13]

Representing the entity

The organization, and not its employees, is the client.

Lawyer employed or retained by an organization represents the organization acting through its duly organized constituents [Rule 1.13(a)].

Rule 1.13(d) requires a lawyer to inform individuals acting for organizations that the organization is their client when there is a possible conflict between individuals and the organization.

Consent of the organization as the client is necessary under Rule 1.7 if the *lawyer represents individuals* in the organization who might have a *conflict of interest with the organization.*

Improper conduct by organizations

Rule 1.13(b) arises when the individual representing the organization is engaged in action, intends to act, or refuses to act in violation of a legal obligation to the organization or in violation of law that might be imputed to the organization, and the action is likely to result in substantial injury to the organization.

In deciding what action to take, the lawyer should consider the seriousness of the violation, scope, and nature of the lawyer's representation, the responsibility of persons involved in the organization, the apparent motivation of persons involved, and the policies of the organization concerning such matters.

If a lawyer decides to proceed, the available remedies, in order of *increasing gravity*, are:

asking persons involved to *reconsider the matter,*

advising that a *separate legal opinion be sought* for presentation to the appropriate authority in the organization, or

referring the matter to a *higher authority* in the organization.

Ultimately, the attorney can take the matter to the board of directors.

If the highest authority refuses to act, the matter is a violation of law, and the refusal to act is likely to result in substantial injury to the organization; *final remedy is resignation* [Rule 1.16].

Notes for active learning

Diminished Capacity Clients [Rule 1.14]

Protective actions

When a client's capacity to make adequately considered decisions concerning representation is diminished, whether because of minority, mental impairment, or other reasons, the lawyer shall maintain a *normal client-lawyer relationship* with the client as reasonably as possible.

When an attorney reasonably believes that the diminished capacity client is at risk of substantial physical, financial, or other harm unless action is taken and cannot adequately act in the client's interest, the lawyer may take *reasonably necessary protective actions*, including *consulting others* with the ability to take action to protect the client.

In appropriate cases, the attorney may seek the appointment of *guardian ad litem*, conservator, or guardian.

Information about representing a client with diminished capacity is protected by Rule 1.6.

When taking protective action, the attorney is *impliedly authorized* under Rule 1.6(a) to reveal information about the client, but only to *the extent reasonably necessary* to *protect client's interests*.

Notes for active learning

Safekeeping Property [Rule 1.15]

Segregating client's property

A lawyer must follow strict rules when holding the property of others.

Attorney must *segregate property* of others from personal assets and *indicate ownership*.

Property other than money belonging to others must be kept in a *secure place*.

Money given to a lawyer in advance for expenses must be placed in the *client's funds account* and can only be used for the purposes for which it was advanced.

A lawyer may deposit the lawyer's funds in a client's trust account to pay bank service charges in that account but only in an *amount necessary* for that purpose.

Client trust accounts

Lawyer shall deposit legal fees and expenses paid in advance into a *client trust account*, to be withdrawn by the lawyer only *as fees are earned or expenses incurred*.

Interest earned on these accounts is used to support legal service organizations, and the lawyer is not required to account for the interest earned on these accounts to their client.

Funds shall be kept in a separate account maintained in the state where the lawyer's office is situated or elsewhere with the consent of the client or third person.

Other property shall be *identified* as such and appropriately *safeguarded*.

Complete records of such account funds and other property shall be kept by the lawyer and preserved for [*five years*] after the termination of representation.

Unearned funds must be returned to the client at the end of the attorney-client relationship.

Property for client

Lawyer must promptly notify client or third person if receiving property belonging to others.

Except as stated in this rule or otherwise permitted by law or by agreement with the client, a lawyer shall *promptly deliver to client* or third person any funds or property that the client or third person is entitled to receive and, upon request by the client or third person, shall promptly render a *full accounting* regarding such property.

When during representation, a lawyer has possession of property in which *two or more* persons (one of whom may be the lawyer) *claim interests*, the property shall be *kept separate* by the lawyer until the dispute is resolved.

Lawyer shall promptly distribute all portions of property for which interests are not disputed.

A lawyer must render an accounting if a client or third party is entitled to an accounting.

Unless permitted by Rules or by agreement, the lawyer must promptly deliver the property to the person entitled to receive it.

Suppose a lawyer receives funds belonging to the client, which are partly owed to the client's creditors. The lawyer may have a duty under applicable *law or agreement* with client to protect creditors and can *withhold money* subject to a creditor's claims from the client.

Funds in dispute

If there is no dispute on the division of the funds, the lawyer must pay the client the amount due and transfer their portion of the funds to their personal account.

If there is a dispute concerning the division of funds, the client and the lawyer can be paid the *amounts undisputedly* due each from the *client's funds account*.

Disputed amounts must remain in the client's funds account *until* dispute is resolved.

Professional responsibility vignette 4

During the last month, the following events occurred at the three-lawyer firm of which you are a partner.

Following a review of the firm's books, its outside accountant informed you and Abby that Paul had used funds kept in the firm's Clients' Trust Fund account ("Account") for personal purposes, resulting in the Account being depleted. On the same day, the firm received a demand from a client that the firm now delivers to him the net proceeds from a completed real estate transaction that had been held in the Account. There are insufficient funds in the Account to meet the client's demand.

Client's funds: a lawyer shall promptly deliver funds the client is entitled to receive [Rule 1:15(b)].

Lawyer can take from client's fund account only funds belonging to lawyer and not client.

Professional misconduct: a lawyer knowing that another lawyer has violated the Rules of Professional Conduct, which raises a substantial question about that lawyer's *honesty, trustworthiness, or fitness*, shall *inform* the appropriate authority [Rule 8.3].

It is *professional misconduct* for a lawyer to conduct *dishonesty or fraud* [Rule 8.4].

Paul embezzled funds from the firm's trust fund account and has violated the disciplinary rule requiring that client funds be promptly delivered to the client.

He has also engaged in acts of *fraud and dishonesty.*

Since you have *unprivileged knowledge* of this act, you *must report* his conduct to the appropriate authority.

Once you and Abby, as other firm members, know that their trust fund account is underfunded, you and Abby should immediately restore funds to the client's fund account, which Paul improperly withdrew.

You should comply with the disciplinary rule and *pay the client promptly* with the funds you restored to the account.

You have a cause of action to *recover funds from Paul.*

Notes for active learning

Terminating Representation [Rule 1.16]

Completed services

A lawyer's representation of a client ordinarily continues to complete the matter.

Rule 1.16 addresses three types of *premature termination* of the relationship:

Discharge by client

Except where a *tribunal orders* the attorney to continue representing the client, the attorney-client relationship is terminated by the client at *will, with or without cause.*

If there is a *binding employment contract*, the lawyer *cannot* specifically enforce it but may sue for *damages for breach of contract.*

If the matter is subject to a *contingent fee agreement*, a suit for *breach* of that agreement must await the *matter's conclusion.*

Mandatory withdrawal

Unless ordered to continue by a tribunal, a lawyer *must withdraw* from representation if continuation of representation will cause the lawyer to *violate Rules of Professional Conduct.*

Attorney *must withdraw* if the lawyer's *physical or mental condition materially impairs* their ability to represent the client.

Permissive withdrawal

Lawyer may withdraw from employment at their option except when prohibited by a tribunal if withdrawal can be accomplished *without material adverse* effect on the client's interests.

With a material adverse effect, the lawyer still *may withdraw* for the following reasons, if:

1) client persists in the course of conduct related to the lawyer's services that the lawyer believes is *criminal or fraudulent*;

2) client has, in the past, used the lawyer's services to perpetrate a *crime or fraud* without knowledge or consent of the lawyer;

3) client insists on pursuing a goal that the lawyer considers in their subjective judgment to be *repugnant or imprudent*;

4) client, after warning, *fails to fulfill obligations* to attorney;

5) continued representation will result in *unreasonable financial* burden to the lawyer;

6) client's actions rendered representation *unreasonably difficult*, or when *another good cause exists*.

Withdrawing lawyer's responsibilities

Attorney *must*

protect client's interest to the greatest extent practical when withdrawing.

give reasonable notice before withdrawing so client obtains substitute counsel.

give client those *papers and property* to which the client is entitled.

refund any portion of the fee which has not been earned.

return papers given by the client, documents such as pleadings filed with the court, all discovery where the client has paid transcript fees, and all research and documents for which *client has paid*.

make available all materials in client's file if failure to do so would *adversely affect* the client even though the lawyer has *not* been fully paid for their services.

Professional responsibility vignette 5

During the last month, the following events occurred at the three-lawyer firm of which you are a partner. Michael, a firm client, has incurred unpaid fees at the firm of $5,000 in connection with the defense of criminal action against him. Your partner Abby is representing him. Shortly after the firm billed Michael, he directed Abby to withdraw her appearance in the case and send the entire original file to his new lawyer. Abby suggested that she tell Michael she will do what he asks after he pays the outstanding bill and requests your opinion on whether she should do so. What answer would you give her?

Attorney withdrawal: a lawyer shall withdraw from representation if lawyer is discharged [Rule 1.16].

If rules require permission for withdrawal from a tribunal, a lawyer shall not withdraw from a proceeding before that tribunal without its permission [Rule 1.16(c)].

Lawyer must make available to a former client within a *reasonable time following* the client's request for their file [Rule 1.16(e)]:

> 1) all papers, documents, or materials supplied to the lawyer.

> 2) all pleadings and papers filed with or by court or served by or upon any party.

> 3) all investigatory or discovery documents for which the client has paid the lawyer's out-of-pocket costs.

> 4) if the lawyer and the client have *not* entered into a contingent fee agreement, the client is entitled only to that *portion of the lawyer's work product* for which the client has paid.

> 5) notwithstanding the contrary, a lawyer may *not refuse*, on the grounds of nonpayment, to make available materials in the client's file when retention would prejudice the client unfairly.

Since this representation involves a court appearance, Abby must obtain permission to withdraw. This should be routine if the new lawyer enters their appearance while filing a motion to withdraw.

Abby cannot pursue the course of action she suggests because she will violate Rule 1.16.

Upon the termination of her employment, she must return to the client all documentation that the client supplied, all court papers which have been filed, all investigatory and discovery documents for which the client has paid the out-of-pocket expenses and any portion of Abby's work product for which the Michael has paid.

In addition, she may not refuse to turn over any material that would prejudice the client in the case. Abby will have to rely on other means to get paid.

Notes for active learning

Sale of Law Practice [Rule 1.17]

Transferring legal practice

Lawyer or law firm *may* sell or purchase a law practice.

The sale must meet the following requirements to *avoid ethical violations* by the firm or lawyers selling or purchasing the practice.

Notifying clients

Attorney must provide *written notice* to clients that the practice is being sold and inform them that they have the *right to retain other counsel* or take *possession of their file*.

Consent to transfer representation will be presumed if they do *not object* within *90 days*.

Changing fees

Purchaser *cannot unilaterally increase* fees charged to clients.

However, the attorney *can refuse* to accept the representation of a particular client unless the client agrees to *pay the fees usually charged* by others for *similar services*.

Notes for active learning

Duties to Prospective Clients [Rule 1.18]

Vetting attorney-client relationship

A person who consults with a lawyer about the possibility of forming a client-attorney relationship for a matter is a *prospective client.*

Even when no client-lawyer relationship ensues, a lawyer who has learned information from a prospective client shall not use or reveal that information, except as Rule 1.9 would permit concerning the information of a former client.

Lawyer shall not represent a client with interests *materially adverse* to those of a prospective client in the same or a substantially related matter if the lawyer receives information from the prospective client that could be significantly harmful to that person.

Disqualified attorney

If a lawyer is disqualified from representation under this rule, *no lawyer* in their firm may knowingly *undertake or continue* representation in such a matter.

When the lawyer has received disqualifying information, representation is permissible if:

1) both *affected client* and *prospective client* have given informed *consent confirmed in writing*, or:

2) lawyer who received information took reasonable measures to *avoid exposure* to more disqualifying information than reasonably necessary to determine whether to represent the prospective client; and

a) disqualified lawyer is timely *screened from participating* in the matter and is apportioned *no part of the fee*; and

b) *written notice* is *promptly* given to *prospective clients.*

Notes for active learning

Chapter 3

Attorney as Counselor

Advisor [Rule 2.1]

Rendering professional judgment

In representing a client, an attorney shall exercise *independent professional judgment* and render *candid advice*.

In rendering advice, an attorney may refer not only to law but to other considerations, such as *moral, economic, social,* and *political factors relevant* to the client's situation.

Client is entitled to straightforward advice expressing the lawyer's honest assessment.

Legal advice involves unpleasant facts and alternatives that a client is unwilling to confront.

Lawyer should consider the client's morale and may *advise as honesty permits*.

However, a lawyer should give *candid advice unpalatable* to the client.

Advice couched in narrow legal terms may be of little value to a client, especially where *practical considerations*, such as cost or effects on others, are *predominant*.

Purely technical legal advice, therefore, can sometimes be *inadequate*.

It is proper for a lawyer to refer to *relevant moral* and *ethical considerations*.

Moral and ethical considerations impinge upon most legal questions and may decisively influence how the law will be applied.

Technical advice

Client may expressly or impliedly ask the lawyer for *strictly technical advice*.

However, when such a request is made by a client *inexperienced in legal matters*, the lawyer's responsibility as advisor indicates that more may be involved than strict legal considerations.

Lawyer's advice often involves recommending a course of action in the face of *conflicting expert recommendations*.

Matters beyond strictly legal questions may be in the domain of another profession.

Where a competent lawyer would recommend consultation with a professional in another field, the lawyer should make such a *recommendation*.

Investigations

Lawyer ordinarily has *no duty to investigate* a client's affairs or *give unwanted advice.*

Lawyer may initiate advice to a client when doing so appears to be in the client's interest.

Unsolicited advice

Generally, a lawyer is *not expected to advise* until the client asks.

However, when a lawyer knows that a client proposes a course of action likely to result in *substantial adverse legal consequences*, the lawyer's duty to the client may *require rendering advice* if the client's course of action is related to the representation.

When a matter is likely to *involve litigation,* it may be necessary to inform the client of forms of *dispute resolution* as alternatives to litigation.

Third Party Evaluations [Rule 2.3]

Client evaluations

Lawyer may evaluate a matter affecting a client for the use of someone other than the client if the lawyer reasonably believes that making the evaluation is *compatible* with other aspects of the lawyer's relationship with the client.

Adverse evaluations

When the lawyer knows or reasonably should know that the evaluation will affect the *client's interests materially and adversely*, the lawyer shall *not* provide the evaluation unless the client gives *informed consent.*

Except as disclosure is authorized in connection with an evaluation report, information relating to the evaluation is otherwise *protected* by Rule 1.6.

Lawyers as Third-Party Neutrals [Rule 2.4]

Dispute resolution

Lawyer serves as a third-party neutral when the lawyer assists *two or more persons* who are *not clients* of the lawyer to resolve a dispute or other matter that has arisen between them.

Service as a third-party neutral may include service as an arbitrator, a mediator, or another capacity enabling the lawyer to assist the parties in resolving the matter.

Informing clients

Lawyer serving as a third-party neutral shall inform unrepresented parties that the lawyer is *not representing* them.

When the lawyer knows or should know that a party does not understand the lawyer's role in the matter, the lawyer shall *explain the differences* between the lawyer's role as a third-party neutral and the lawyer's role as one who represents a client.

Notes for active learning

Chapter 4

Attorney as Advocate

Frivolous Claims or Defenses Prohibited [Rule 3.1]

Good faith arguments

Rule 3 imposes ethical obligations on lawyers engaging in litigation.

Rule 3.1 provides that in civil actions, a lawyer shall not bring or defend a proceeding or assert or controvert an issue therein unless there is a *basis* for doing so that is *not frivolous*, which includes a *good faith argument* for extension, modification, or reversal of existing law.

Operative disciplinary standard under Rule 3.1 is "frivolous."

If a lawyer asserts a claim or defense *not based* on existing law or reasonable likelihood of a change in existing law, then the claim or defense is *frivolous*.

Action is frivolous, even though there is a good faith belief that it will succeed if brought *primarily to harass* or *maliciously injure* a person.

Criminal Defense Standards

Prosecutor's burden

Attorney for a defendant in a *criminal proceeding* that could require *incarceration* can require the *prosecution to prove every element* of its case even though the same actions by a lawyer in a *civil case* could be considered *frivolous*.

Expediting Litigation [Rule 3.2]

Timely prosecution

Lawyers must make reasonable efforts to *expedite litigation consistent* with client's interest. [Rule 3.2]

Notes for active learning

Obligations to Tribunals [Rule 3.3]

Misrepresentations

Lawyer shall not knowingly make false representations of *fact or law* to a tribunal [Rule 3.3(a)(1)].

Disclosing facts

Lawyer has an *affirmative duty to disclose material facts* to a tribunal when disclosure is necessary to avoid assisting a criminal or fraudulent act by the client, except when Rule 3.3 prevents such disclosure [Rule 3.3(a)(3)].

Controlling authority

Lawyer has the *affirmative duty to cite* to the court legal authority controlling the jurisdiction known to the lawyer to be directly *adverse* to the position of the client and *not* disclosed by the opposing counsel [Rule 3.3(a)(2)].

Presenting facts

Lawyer may *not offer* evidence known to be false and may refuse to offer evidence that the lawyer reasonably believes is false *even if client directs* them to offer it [Rule 3.3(a)(3)].

If the attorney has already offered evidence or the lawyer's client or witness testifying on behalf of the client has given material evidence, and the lawyer comes to know of its falsity, the lawyer must take *reasonable remedial measures*.

Duty to take *reasonable remedial measures* continues to the conclusion of the proceeding, including appeals, and applies *even if* compliance requires *disclosure of information protected* under the *confidentiality provisions* of Rule 1.6.

Lawyer may submit pleadings and other documents to the tribunal based upon knowledge *obtained from client*, which *appears truthful* and need *not* make independent inquiry into truth of the facts.

However, suppose a lawyer gives an affidavit or asserts a statement is of their knowledge. In that case, they must *either know* the statement to be true or *believe* it to be accurate based on *reasonably diligent inquiry*.

Ex Parte proceedings

In an *ex parte* proceeding, a lawyer shall inform the tribunal of *material facts known*, enabling the tribunal to decide whether the facts are adverse [Rule 3.3(d)].

Criminal cases

In a criminal case, defense counsel who knows that the defendant, the client, intends *to testify falsely* may *not aid the client* in constructing false testimony and has a *duty strongly to discourage* the client from testifying falsely, advising the client such a course is *unlawful* and will have *substantial adverse consequences* and should *not* be followed.

If the lawyer discovers this intention before accepting representation of the client, the lawyer shall *not accept* the representation.

If the lawyer discovers this intention before trial, the lawyer shall *withdraw* from the representation, requesting any required permission.

Privileged or prejudicial information shall be disclosed only to the extent necessary to affect the withdrawal.

Suppose disclosure of privileged or prejudicial information is necessary. In that case, the lawyer shall apply to withdraw *ex parte* to a judge other than the judge who will preside at the trial and shall seek to be heard *in camera* and have the record of the proceeding, except for an order granting leave to withdraw, *impounded.*

The lawyer may *not prevent client* from testifying if the lawyer cannot obtain the required permission to withdraw.

Suppose a criminal trial has commenced, and the lawyer discovers that the client intends to testify falsely. In that case, the lawyer need not file a motion to withdraw from the case if the lawyer reasonably believes that *seeking to withdraw will prejudice* the client.

During the client's testimony, or after the client has testified, the lawyer knows that the client has testified falsely. In that case, the *lawyer shall call* upon the client to *rectify false testimony*. If the client refuses or cannot do so, the lawyer shall *not reveal* the false testimony to the tribunal.

In no event may the lawyer examine the client to *elicit testimony* from the client the lawyer knows to be *false.*

Lawyer shall *not argue the probative value* of false testimony in *closing arguments* or other *proceedings*, including appeals.

Opposing Party and Counsel [Rule 3.4]

Fairness during litigation

Rule 3.4 imposes ethical standards on counsel interacting with opposing parties and counsel.

Rules apply once litigation has *commenced.*

Quest for evidence

Lawyer is prohibited from obstructing another's access to evidence or counseling others to do the same [Rule 3.4(a)].

Lawyer cannot alter, destroy, or conceal a document having *evidentiary value.*

Rules must be viewed in the context of *adversarial litigation.*

Absent litigation, a lawyer may counsel clients to destroy records routinely.

Once litigation has begun, a lawyer or a client acting under a lawyer's instructions cannot *systematically purge files* of harmful documents even though discovery has *not begun.*

Witnesses

Lawyer is prohibited from falsifying evidence or counseling, assisting a witness to testify falsely, or offering an inducement to a witness prohibited by law [Rule 3.4(b)].

However, a lawyer ordinarily has *no obligation to help an opponent find witnesses.*

Lawyer is *prohibited from paying* a witness compensation as an inducement [Rule 3.4(b)].

However, under that rule, a *lawyer can pay* a witness:

1) *expenses reasonably incurred* by a witness in attending or testifying;

2) *reasonable compensation* to a witness for loss of time in attending or testifying;

3) *reasonable fee* for a professional or expert witness.

Discovery

When engaging in pretrial procedure, a lawyer cannot make a *frivolous discovery request* or *fail to make* a reasonably diligent effort to comply with the opposing party's legally proper discovery requests [Rule 3.4(d)].

Preventing opposing party from voluntarily obtaining information

Lawyer cannot request that a person *other than a client* refrain from voluntarily giving relevant information to another party unless the person is a *relative, employee, or agent* of client and the lawyer believes that that person's interests *will not* be adversely affected by refraining from giving such information [Rule 3.4(f)].

Complying with court rules

Lawyer cannot knowingly *disobey an obligation* under the rules of a tribunal except for an *open refusal* based on an assertion that no valid obligation exists [Rule 3.4(f)].

Litigation statements

Lawyer, while trying a case, *cannot* [Rule 3.4(e)]:

1) allude to any matter that the lawyer does not reasonably believe is *relevant* or that will not be supported by *admissible evidence*.

2) assert personal knowledge of facts in issue *except when testifying* as a witness, and

3) state an opinion as to the *justness of a cause, witness credibility, culpability of a civil litigant,* or *guilt or innocence* of the accused.

However, in final arguments, lawyers may *analyze evidence presented* and *suggest inferences* that the finder of fact can draw from the evidence.

Professional responsibility vignette 6

A former employee sued Paul's client for racial discrimination. Paul has asked whether he may tell certain potential witnesses to the case (the members of the client's Board of Directors, the client's current and former employees, and a few customers of the client) not to talk to the former employee's attorney if she calls them seeking information.

Obstructing quest for evidence: a lawyer shall not request a person other than a client to refrain from voluntarily giving relevant information to another party unless the:

1) person is a relative or an employee, or an agent of the client *and*

2) lawyer reasonably believes that the person's interests will not be adversely affected by refraining from giving such information [Rule 3.4(f)].

Lawyer is prohibited from requesting that a person other than a client refrain from voluntarily giving relevant information to another party unless the person is a relative or an employee, or other agents of the client or the lawyer reasonably believes that the person's interest will be adversely affected by refraining from giving such information.

Under the rule, Paul may tell members of the client's board of directors and current employees not to talk to the former employee's attorney.

Paul may not make the same request of former employees or customers unless he reasonably believes their interests will be adversely affected by talking to the employee's lawyer.

Professional responsibility vignette 7

A lawyer represented the Buyer in a suit for breach of contract by the Seller to sell a residential home to the Buyer. In conferences in preparing the case, the Buyer made the following requests to the lawyer:

When having a witness subpoena served on the real estate broker, in addition to the statutory fee and expenses required to be paid, the lawyer should pay him $3,700 "to show we value highly the time he will be spending in court and away from his business."

Prohibited witness payments: a lawyer may not pay (i.e., offer inducements) lay witnesses, except for reasonable expenses involved in testifying and reasonable compensation for loss of time in attending and testifying [Rule 3.4(b)].

Proposed payment of $3,700 seems designed to influence testimony. It does not seem to bear a reasonable relation to compensation the real estate broker should be paid for lost time.

Value of broker's time must be based upon the *market value* of his services, *not* the subjective value of a party to the lawsuit.

Lawyer should *only pay* the witness for his *expenses* and the *value of his time.*

Professional responsibility vignette 8

Amy represented the Buyer in a suit for breach of contract by the Seller to sell a residential home to the Buyer. In conferences in preparation for the case, the Buyer made the following requests to the lawyer: Amy should arrange for the Buyer's secretary, who took notes at the conferences between the Buyer and Seller, to be out of the state during any scheduled trial dates so that she could not be subpoenaed as a witness.

Obstructing access to evidence: a lawyer is prohibited from unlawfully obstructing another party's access to evidence.

Causing the buyer's secretary, who can testify to relevant substantial evidence, to leave the state so that she cannot be subpoenaed as a witness at trial violates this rule.

Lawyer should decline to arrange for the secretary to be out of state during the trial and not counsel his client, the Buyer, to make such arrangements [Rule 3.4(a)].

Impartiality and Decorum of Tribunal [Rule 3.5]

Ex parte communications

Lawyer shall not influence a judge, juror, potential juror, or public official by means prohibited by law and from communicating *ex parte* except as permitted by law [Rule 3.5].

Contacting jurors

Lawyer's contact with jurors, prospective jurors, and members of jurors' families is regulated before, during, and after the trial.

Before trial, a lawyer connected with a case, the lawyer's client, and persons working for the lawyer are *prohibited from communicating* with anyone they know to be a member of the *venire* from which the jury will be chosen.

Lawyers may investigate potential jurors for bias and learn about their backgrounds.

Investigation must not be vexatious or harassing; juror's family cannot be contacted.

During the trial, a lawyer may communicate with jurors *only in the courtroom*, following the *rules established* for the trial of cases.

After the jury has been discharged from further deliberations, a lawyer connected with the case may *not initiate* communications with the jurors without *leave of court for a good cause*.

Suppose the juror initiates communication directly or indirectly. In that case, the lawyer may respond, provided that a lawyer shall not ask questions or make comments to a jury member intended only to *harass or embarrass* the juror or *influence* their actions in future jury service.

In *no circumstances* shall such a lawyer *inquire* of jurors concerning *the deliberation process*.

Communicating with judges

In a non-adversarial proceeding, such as the probate of most estates, a lawyer is permitted to contact the tribunal without limitation by the Rules.

In adversarial proceedings, a lawyer may communicate with tribunals during official proceedings.

Outside official proceedings, the lawyer may communicate with the *judge in writing* if the lawyer promptly delivers a *copy to opposing counsel* (or opposing party if counsel does not represent that party).

If the lawyer desires to *communicate orally*, the lawyer must give notice of the time of the oral communication to opposing counsel or opponent if unrepresented.

Preserving decorum

Lawyer must *preserve decorum* of tribunal by refraining from disruptive actions [Rule 3.5(c)].

Trial Publicity [Rule 3.6]

Fair trial *vs.* free expression rights

Rule 3.6 balances the right to a *fair trial* and *right to free expression*.

To protect the right to a fair trial, the jury must be shielded from information that might cause *prejudgment* or consideration of *evidence inadmissible* at trial.

However, First Amendment rights must be protected.

Public has a right to know about threats to its safety and the measures taken to protect it.

Public has a right to know about judicial proceedings.

Public has a right to participate in questions about public policy, which are often raised in those proceedings.

Extrajudicial statements

Rule 3.6 is applicable when a lawyer either talks to the media with the reasonable expectation that the statement will be published or acts in a way that makes it likely that the information will be disseminated.

Protected statements

Lawyer can disseminate the following types of statements to the *media* without violating the rule (provided they are stated without elaboration) [Rule 3.6(c)]:

1) general nature of the claim or defense;

2) information contained in the public record;

3) that an investigation is in progress, general scope of the investigation, offense or defense involved, and, except where prohibited by law (e.g., the suspect is a juvenile), the identity of persons involved;

4) *scheduling* or a *result* of any step in litigation;

5) request assistance to obtain evidence or information for that request;

6) a warning of danger concerning the behavior of a person involved, where there is reason to believe that there exists the *likelihood of substantial harm* to an individual or the public,

7) in a criminal case, the following information may be disseminated (a statement that a defendant has been charged with a crime must include a statement explaining that the charge is merely an *accusation* and that the defendant is *presumed innocent* until and unless proven guilty):

---

a) identity, residence, occupation, and family status of the accused;

b) if the accused has not been apprehended, information necessary to aid in the apprehension of that person;

c) fact, time, and place of arrest; and

d) identity of investigating and arresting officers and length of the investigation.

Prohibited statements

Statements to the media prohibited under Rule 3.6(a) are those unprotected statements that a lawyer knows or reasonably should know will have a substantial likelihood of *materially prejudicing* an adjudicative proceeding.

In a civil matter tried before a jury or criminal matter or proceeding which may result in incarceration, the following statements ordinarily have effects *prohibited* by Rule 3.6(a); that is, they have a substantial likelihood of *materially prejudicing an adjudicative proceeding*:

1) character, credibility, reputation, or criminal record of a party or witness;

2) identity of a witness;

3) expected testimony of a party or witness;

4) possibility of a plea of guilty in a criminal case;

5) existence or contents of a confession or statement given by defendant or suspect;

6) that the defendant or suspect refused to make a statement;

7) performance or results of any examination or test;

8) refusal or failure of a person to submit to an examination or test;

9) identity or nature of any physical evidence expected to be presented;

10) opinion of the guilt or innocence of a defendant or suspect in a criminal case;

11) evidence that the lawyer knows *inadmissible at trial,* and which would create a *substantial risk of prejudicing* an impartial trial if disclosed; and

12) the defendant has been charged with a crime unless accompanied by a statement that the charge is merely an *accusation,* and defendant is *presumed innocent* until proven guilty.

Controlling others

Defense attorneys and prosecutors must use reasonable care to prevent staff, investigators, law enforcement, employees, and others *under their control* from making statements prohibited by Rule 3.6.

Responding to attacks

Rule 3.6 does *not* preclude a lawyer from *responding to attacks publicly made* against them.

Professional responsibility vignette 9

A lawyer represented the Buyer in a suit for breach of contract by the Seller to sell a residential home to the Buyer. In conferences to prepare the case, the Buyer made the following requests to the lawyer:

The lawyer should place an advertisement in the local newspaper describing the case and asking for persons to contact him with evidence of the established custom by the Seller to refuse to go through with real estate sales to procure more than the agreed-upon sales price.

Extrajudicial statements: A lawyer is prohibited from extra-judicial statements disseminated using publication if a lawyer knows it will have a substantial likelihood of materially prejudicing the adjudication [Rule 3.6].

Seller's activity in other transactions is probably inadmissible and does not establish a custom. It is not engaged in with such regularity that it constitutes habit evidence.

Methods exist to investigate the seller's past business dealings *without* public advertisement.

Therefore, the purpose of such an advertisement could not be to seek admissible evidence.

If the effect of this advertisement would be to acquaint potential jurors with knowledge of the past inadmissible behavior of the seller, it could violate Rule 3.6.

Lawyer should advise his client that he will *not* place the advertisement.

Notes for active learning

Lawyer as Witness [Rule 3.7]

Advocacy prohibited

Rule 3.7(a) prevents a lawyer from serving as an advocate when likely to be a necessary witness *except* when the:

1) issue on which the lawyer is to testify is *not contested*;

2) issue is the extent and value of the *lawyer's services*; or

3) disqualification of the lawyer would cause *substantial hardship to client* and court must examine the circumstances.

Firm not disqualified

Unless there is a conflict of interest as described below, there is *no imputed disqualification* of members of witness-lawyer's firm if the witness-lawyer is disqualified from trying the case.

Lawyers in the firm *may try a case* in which another firm *lawyer is a witness*.

Notes for active learning

Prosecutor Responsibilities [Rule 3.8]

Probable cause requirement

Prosecutor shall refrain from prosecuting a charge the prosecutor knows *is not supported by probable cause* [Rule 3.8(a)].

Prosecutor shall make reasonable efforts to ensure that the accused has been advised of the right to obtain counsel and has been given reasonable *opportunity to obtain counsel* [Rule 3.8(b)].

Prosecutor shall not obtain a waiver of important pretrial rights from an unrepresented defendant unless the court has first obtained a knowing and intelligent written waiver of their right to counsel [Rule 3.8(c)].

Mitigating factors

Prosecutors have the *constitutional obligation* to make *timely disclosure* to the accused or to their counsel information in possession of the prosecutor's office, which would *negate* the guilt of the accused or *mitigate* the degree of the offense [Rule 3.8(d)].

At sentencing, the prosecutor must disclose to the tribunal and the defense *all unprivileged information* that would tend to *mitigate the sentence* [Rule 3.8(d)].

Prosecutors may seek relief from these disclosure responsibilities by obtaining a *protective order* from the tribunal [Rule 3.8(d)].

Counsel testimony

Prosecutor shall *not subpoena* a *lawyer to present evidence* about a current or former client unless the prosecutor reasonably believes (and after a hearing at which the lawyer has an opportunity to be heard and the *judge concurs*) that the information sought is [Rule 3.8(e)]:

   1) *not privileged,*

   2) *essential* to the case, and

   3) *not* otherwise *reasonably obtainable,* or the prosecutor obtains *prior* judicial approval after an opportunity for an *adversarial hearing.*

Extrajudicial statements

Except for statements that are necessary to inform the public of the nature and extent of the prosecutor's action and that serve a legitimate law enforcement purpose, refrain from making extrajudicial comments that have a substantial likelihood of heightening public condemnation of the accused and exercise reasonable care to prevent other persons associated with the prosecutor in a criminal case from making an extrajudicial statement that the prosecutor would be prohibited from making under Rule 3.6 or this Rule [Rule 3.8(f)].

Exculpatory evidence

Prosecutors knowing of *new, material evidence* creating a reasonable likelihood that a convicted defendant did not commit an offense of which the *defendant was convicted* shall [Rule 3.8(g)]:

> 1) promptly disclose that evidence to an appropriate court or authority, and

> 2) if the conviction was obtained in the prosecutor's jurisdiction,

>> i) promptly *disclose evidence* to the defendant unless a court authorizes delay, and

>> ii) undertake a *further investigation* or make reasonable efforts to cause an investigation, to determine whether the defendant was convicted of an offense that the *defendant did not commit.*

Wrongful convictions

When a prosecutor knows of *clear and convincing evidence* that a defendant in the prosecutor's jurisdiction was convicted of an offense the defendant did *not commit*, the prosecutor shall seek to *remedy the conviction* [Rule 3.8(h)].

Advocate in Non-adjudicative Proceedings [Rule 3.9]

Obligations of candor and decorum

Rule 3.9 imposes upon lawyers appearing before *non-adjudicative tribunals* the same *obligations of candor* as to *law* and *fact* imposed by Rule 3.3(a)(1), the obligation to

act fairly for access to evidence imposed by Rules 3.4(a) and 3.4(b),

obey the rules of the tribunal imposed by Rule 3.4(c), and

secure impartiality and decorum of the tribunal imposed by Rule 3.5.

Governmental appearances

When a lawyer engages in bilateral negotiations with a government agency, the Rules on dealings with persons other than clients (Rules 4.1 through 4.4) are substituted for the rule governing appearances before a tribunal.

Notes for active learning

Chapter 5

Transactions with Third Persons

Truthful Statements [Rule 4.1]

Veracity and disclosure

Lawyer is prohibited from knowingly making a *false statement of material fact* to a third person and *failing to disclose material facts* to a third person when disclosure is necessary to avoid assisting a criminal or fraudulent act by the client [Rule 4.1(a)].

There is no obligation to disclose when disclosure is *prohibited* by Rule 1.6, which imposes an *obligation of confidentiality* on a lawyer.

Communicating with Represented Persons [Rule 4.2]

Permitted communications

Rule 4.2 prohibits a lawyer representing a client from communicating about the subject representation with a person the lawyer knows to be represented by another unless the lawyer has the other lawyer's consent or is authorized by law.

Professional responsibility vignette 10

Cheryl admitted confidentially to her attorney Lynne that she lied at her deposition concerning the extent of her physical and emotional injuries. Based chiefly on that testimony, Robert offered to settle the case for $100,000, far beyond Lynne's estimate of the claim's value. Robert delivered a check in that amount to Lynne payable to "Lynne, as the attorney for Cheryl." Cheryl accepted the offer.

Misrepresentation: a lawyer is prohibited from knowingly making a false statement of material fact and failing to disclose a material fact to a third person when disclosure is necessary to avoid assisting a criminal or fraudulent act by the client [Rule 4.1(a)].

No obligation to disclose when *disclosure is prohibited* by Rule 1.6, which imposes an *obligation of confidentiality* on a lawyer.

Before negotiating the settlement with Robert, Lynne knew that Cheryl lied about the extent of her injuries in the deposition. These statements formed the basis of the extent of Cheryl's injuries for settlement negotiations.

Even though these statements were privileged when made to Lynne, they were not privileged when used to obtain a settlement that defrauded Robert because of the false nature of Lynne's deposition testimony.

Lynne violated Rule 4.1(b) when she failed to disclose a *material fact* to a third person where *disclosure is necessary to avoid* assisting a *fraudulent act* by a client.

Notes for active learning

Communicating with Unrepresented Persons [Rule 4.3]

Misunderstandings

Lawyer can communicate with a person with opposing interests whom counsel does not represent but cannot state or imply that they are disinterested [Rule 4.3(a)].

When a lawyer knows or reasonably should know that the *unrepresented person misunderstands* the lawyer's role in the matter, lawyer shall make *reasonable efforts* to correct the misunderstanding.

Lawyer *cannot* give legal advice to an *unrepresented person.*

Instead, the lawyer must advise such unrepresented person to *seek legal counsel* [Rule 4.3(b)].

Respecting Rights of Third Persons [Rule 4.4]

Civility and meaningful purpose

Lawyers must treat third *persons with respect*, whether adversaries or merely persons involved in representing their clients.

Lawyers cannot use means that have no purpose other than to *embarrass, delay or burden third partie*s or use means of *obtaining evidence violating* the legal rights of such a person.

Notes for active learning

Chapter 6

Law Firms and Associations

Supervisory Lawyer's Responsibilities [Rule 5.1]

Duty of oversight

Partners in a law firm shall make *reasonable efforts* to ensure that the firm has measures assuring lawyers in the firm *conform* to the Rules of Professional Conduct [Rule 5.1(a)].

Imputed Violations

Ratifying conduct

A lawyer, whether or not that lawyer is in a supervisory position, is responsible for a violation of the Rules of Professional Conduct if another *lawyer or a non-lawyer-employee* commits a violation of the Rules and the lawyer *either orders the conduct or knows* of the specific conduct, ratifies the conduct [Rule 5.1(c)(1) and 5.3(c)(1)].

Duty to mitigate

A lawyer, who is either a partner in the law firm where a lawyer or non-lawyer is employed or is the direct supervisor of such person, is responsible for a violation of the Rules of Professional Conduct if the lawyer or *non-lawyer-employee* commits a violation of the Rules and the lawyer knows of the conduct when its consequences can be *avoided or mitigated* but *fails to take reasonable remedial actions* [Rules 5.1(c)(2) and 5.3(c)(2)].

Subordinate Lawyer's Responsibilities [Rule 5.2]

Subordinates bound

Subordinate lawyer is bound by the Rules of Professional Conduct *even when acting* at the direction of another [Rule 5.2(a)].

Reasonable resolutions

However, a subordinate lawyer does not violate the Rules of Professional Conduct if the lawyer acts following a supervisory lawyer's *reasonable resolution of an arguable question* of professional duty [Rule 5.2(b)].

Duty extends to a lawyer having *supervisory authority* over another lawyer [Rule 5.2(b)].

Notes for active learning

Non-Lawyer Responsibilities [Rule 5.3]

Duty to supervise

Same duty for adherence to Rules of Professional Conduct extends to *partners* and lawyers in a law firm having *supervision over non-lawyers* employed, retained, or associated with firm [Rule 5.3].

Professional Independence of Lawyer [Rule 5.4]

Non-lawyer estate

Lawyer may *not share a fee* with a *non-lawyer* except that a lawyer and their firm can, by agreement, provide that upon the *lawyer's death*, the firm will pay the *lawyer's estate* or one or more designated individual's money over a *reasonable period* [Rule 5.4(a)(1)].

Non-lawyer purchase

Lawyer may purchase the practice of a deceased, disabled, or disappeared lawyer at the agreed-upon purchase price for the practice [Rule 5.4(a)(2)].

Non-lawyer retirement

Lawyer may include law firm employees in a compensation or retirement program even though the money paid into the program is based upon the profit of the firm [Rule 5.4(a)(3)].

Non-lawyer partnership

Lawyer *cannot form a partnership* with a *non-lawyer* if the partnership's activity consists of the practice of law [Rule 5.4(b)].

Similar limitations for non-lawyers are placed upon professional corporations.

Stockholders must be lawyers except for temporary ownership of a deceased lawyer's estate.

Independent legal judgments

Officers and directors must be *lawyers*.

Non-lawyer *shall not* have the right to direct or control the professional judgment of lawyers working for the corporation.

Lawyer cannot permit the person who *recommends them or pays the fee* to direct or regulate the *lawyer's professional judgment* in rendering legal services [Rule 5.4(c)].

Notes for active learning

Unauthorized Practice of Law [Rule 5.5]

Jurisdiction requirement

Lawyer shall *not practice law* in a jurisdiction when doing so violates the regulation of the legal profession in that jurisdiction [Rule 5.5(a)].

Assisting others not admitted

Lawyer shall *not assist* a person who is not a member of the bar in performing an activity that constitutes the unauthorized practice of law [Rule 5.5(a)].

Delegation of tasks

Lawyer may delegate tasks to non-lawyers without violating the Rules of Professional Conduct, providing the lawyer:

1) maintains a direct relationship with the client;

2) supervises the delegated work; and

3) retains complete professional responsibility for the work.

Systemic contacts

Lawyer *not admitted* to practice in a jurisdiction *shall not* [Rule 5.5(b)]:

1) except as authorized by these Rules or law, establish a *systematic and continuous presence* for the practice of law; or

2) *hold out* to public or *represent admission* to practice law in jurisdiction.

Temporary legal services

Lawyer admitted in a jurisdiction *may* provide legal services *temporarily if* [Rule 5.5(c)]:

1) undertaken *in association* with a lawyer admitted to practice and who *actively participates* in the matter;

2) reasonably related to a *proceeding before a tribunal* if the lawyer or other is authorized to appear in such proceedings;

3) reasonably related to *alternative resolution proceedings*, if the services are reasonably related and do not require *pro hac vice* admission; or

4) reasonably related to lawyer's practice in a *jurisdiction where admitted*.

Organizational affiliation

Lawyer admitted in another jurisdiction *may provide* legal services through an office or *systematic and continuous presence* in the jurisdiction [Rule 5.5(d)]:

> 1) the lawyer's employer or its organizational affiliates are not services for which the forum requires *pro hac vice* admission, and when *performed by the advice of a lawyer duly licensed* by the jurisdiction to provide such advice; or
>
> 2) services the lawyer is authorized by *federal law* in the jurisdiction.

Provided that the following:

> 1) foreign lawyer is a member in *good standing* of a recognized legal profession with the member admitted to practice and regulated by a duly constituted authority; or,
>
> 2) person otherwise lawfully practicing as an *in-house counsel* under the laws of a foreign jurisdiction *must be authorized* to practice under this Rule by the *highest court of this jurisdiction*.

Practice Restrictions [Rule 5.6]

Agreements restricting employment

Non-competition employment agreements between lawyers *are prohibited* [Rule 5.6(a)].

Non-competition for retirement

Any such agreement, *even if limited to a brief time*, to a particular *locality*, or even to *clients of the firm*, is prohibited except that parties can agree that *retirement benefits will be forfeited* if an attorney enters into competition after leaving the former firm's employment.

Restricting practice by settlement

A lawyer is not permitted to agree not to represent other persons as part of a claim settlement even if the client would receive a substantially larger settlement offer because the lawyer agrees to restrict their practice [Rule 5.6(b)].

Professional responsibility vignette 11

Mary has asked whether she may solicit the legal business of a client of her former law firm by sending a short letter announcing her new practice at your law firm. Mary was hired by your law firm right after leaving a nearby firm two weeks ago. As a partner at that law firm, Mary signed a partnership agreement that she would not practice law anywhere for six months if she ever left that law firm

Agreements restricting employment: a lawyer shall not participate in offering or making a *partnership* or *employment agreement* restricting the right of a lawyer to practice after terminating the relationship *except* an agreement concerning *benefits upon retirement* [Rule 5.6].

Jan's agreement with former partners restricting her right to practice is *unenforceable.*

Mary should contact her former partners, and they should *rescind* that provision of her former partnership agreement to *avoid violating* the Rules of Professional Responsibility.

Mary *may* send the announcement letter.

Professional responsibility vignette 12

During the last month, the following events occurred at the three-lawyer firm of which you are a partner. Your partner Paul has told you and Abby that he intends to withdraw from the firm to become a partner at a prominent firm in the same city. When the three of you formed the firm, you entered into a written partnership agreement that provided, in part, as follows:

"If any partner should withdraw from the firm voluntarily, they shall not practice law within this city for one year from and after the withdrawal date."

Paul has asked you and Abby to waive that provision. What answer will you give Paul?

Agreements restricting employment: a lawyer shall not participate in offering or making a partnership agreement that restricts the right of a lawyer to practice after termination of the relationship except in an agreement concerning benefits upon retirement [Rule 5.6].

Partnership agreement, as it presently exists, *violates* disciplinary Rule 5.6.

Partners should *delete the provision* from the partnership agreement and waive any restriction which might affect Paul's future employment.

Law-Related Services [Rule 5.7]

Supervising non-legal services

If a lawyer engages in law-related services, which can be performed in conjunction with legal services but can be performed by *non-lawyers*, the lawyer is subject to the Rules of Professional Responsibility *if not distinct* from legal services.

Entity disclosures

If a lawyer performs services in a separate entity, they are *subject to the Rules* unless it is *clear to consumers* that the lawyer is *not performing legal services* and *protections* of the lawyer-client relationship do not exist.

Notes for active learning

Chapter 7

Public Service

Pro Bono Service [Rule 6.1]

Voluntary legal services

Lawyers have a professional responsibility to provide legal services to those *unable to pay*.

Lawyers should aspire to render *at least fifty* (50) hours of *pro bono* legal services *per year*.

Rendering services

In fulfilling this responsibility, the lawyer should:

Provide a *substantial majority of fifty* (50) hours of legal services without fee to:

> 1) persons of *limited means* or
>
> 2) charitable organizations in matters *for persons of limited means*; and

Provide *additional services* through:

> 1) legal services at *no fee or substantially reduced fee* where the payment of standard legal fees would significantly hinder representation;
>
> 2) legal services at a reduced fee to persons of *limited means*; or
>
> 3) *activities for improving* the law, legal system, or legal profession.

Supporting organizations helping the needy

Lawyers should *voluntarily contribute financial support* to organizations providing legal services to persons of limited means.

Notes for active learning

Accepting Appointments [Rule 6.2]

Duty to represent

Lawyer shall not avoid appointment by tribunal to represent persons except for good cause, such as:

a) representing the client is likely to result in *violating* the Rules of Professional Conduct or other law;

b) representing client will result in an *unreasonable financial burden*; or

c) client or cause is *repugnant* to lawyer, *impairs* the client-lawyer relationship or lawyer's *ability to represent the client*.

Legal Services Memberships [Rule 6.3]

Service not aligned with client

Lawyer may serve as a member of a *legal services organization*, apart from a law firm, even an organization serving persons with *interests adverse* to lawyer's clients.

Actions adverse to clients

Lawyer *shall not participate* in actions of the organization:

a) if participating is contrary to the lawyer's obligations to clients under Rule 1.7; or

b) where actions may have a material *adverse effect* on representation of clients of the organization with interests adverse to the *lawyer's client*.

Notes for active learning

Law Reform Affecting Clients [Rule 6.4]

Contrary organizational objectives

Lawyer *may serve* in an organization involved in *law reform* even if it affects the interests of the lawyer's client.

Disclosing conflicts

When a participating lawyer knows that a decision may benefit a client's interests, the lawyer *shall disclose* that fact but *not identify* the client.

Nonprofit and Limited Legal Services [Rule 6.5]

Limited representation

Lawyer under a program sponsored by a nonprofit or court providing short-term limited legal services without expectation by the lawyer or client of additional representation [Rule 6.5(a)]:

> 1) subject to Rules 1.7 and 1.9(a) *only if lawyer* knows that representation involves a *conflict of interest*; and

> 2) subject to Rule 1.10 only if the lawyer knows that an associated lawyer in the law firm is disqualified by Rule 1.7 or 1.9(a).

Except as provided in Rule 1.10(a)(2) is inapplicable to the representation under this Rule.

Notes for active learning

Chapter 8

Legal Services

Promoting Services [Rule 7.1]

False or misleading advertising

The general restriction on communications by lawyers about the lawyer or services, which applies to communications, including advertising, is that they *shall not be false or misleading.*

Material misrepresentations

Statement is misleading if it contains a *material misrepresentation of fact* or *law*, if,

> *omits facts* considered necessary to make the statement, considered as a whole, not materially misleading;

> likely creates *unjustified expectations* about the results that the lawyer can achieve if it states or implies that a lawyer can achieve results by violating the Rules of Professional Conduct or other law; or

> lawyer compares their services to those of others unless the *comparison factually substantiated.*

Notes for active learning

Advertising [Rule 7.2]

Medium

There are *few limitations* on a lawyer's right to advertise if the communication content complies with Rule 7.1 and the communication does not cross the line between advertising and solicitation regulated by Rule 7.3.

Rules permit advertising if the communication is *not misleading* per Rule 7.1.

Lawyer may use print media, billboards, radio, television, web pages, and electronic or direct mail communications.

If not misleading, *no standards of taste or dignity are imposed* upon the advertising.

Payments

Except for exceptions below, a lawyer may *not pay a person for recommending* that lawyer's legal services [Rule 7.1(b)].

> Lawyer may pay for advertising space in media outlets and may pay those who prepare the advertising, including professional advertising agencies and staff.

> Lawyer may pay for prepaid legal services plans.

> Legal aid agencies may advertise legal services under their auspices and hire lawyers to perform that work.

> Lawyers may pay a *nonprofit lawyer referral service*, many of which are operated by bar associations, the usual fee charged for referred clients.

> Lawyer may purchase a law practice as agreed, per Rule 1.17.

Referral fees

Lawyer *shall not compensate* a person for recommending the lawyer's services except that a lawyer may *refer others by agreement not prohibited if* the:

> 1) *reciprocal referral agreement* is *not exclusive*; and

> 2) *client is informed* of the nature of the agreement [Rule 7.1(b)].

Lawyers may give *nominal gifts of appreciation* as reasonably expected compensation for recommending a lawyer's services.

Certifications

Lawyer shall *not imply certification* in a particular field of law unless:

1) lawyer has been certified as a specialist by the *state bar* or accredited by the *American Bar Association*; and

2) name of *certifying organization is clearly identified* [Rule 7.2(c)].

Disclosures

Communications regulated by this rule must include the *name* and *contact information* of at least *one lawyer* responsible for its content [Rule 7.2(d)].

Solicitation [Rule 7.3]

Prospective clients

Solicitation is *personal contact* with prospective clients for employment concerning a matter [Rule 7.3(a)].

Forbidden solicitation

Lawyer shall *not solicit* professional employment from prospective clients in person, by telephone, or personal contact when lawyer's motive is *personal gain* [Rule 7.3(b)] *unless* the contact is a:

    1) *lawyer*;

    2) person with a personal or *prior relationship* with the lawyer or law firm; or

    3) person who *routinely uses* legal services offered by the lawyer.

Lawyer shall not engage a personal contact, where the client must respond to the lawyer's overtures, fraught with the possibility of *undue influence*, *intimidation*, or *overreaching*, even if the lawyer complies with Rule 7.1 and engages in no misrepresentations [Rule 7.1(c)].

Written communication not using personal contact offering legal services is permitted.

Exceptions

Constitutional limits exist for a ban on in-person solicitation.

Solicitation of prospective litigants by *nonprofit organizations* that engage in litigation as a form of *political expression* and association constitutes expressive and associational conduct *protected* under First Amendment.

Exceptions to the rule banning solicitation:

    Lawyer may solicit relatives and former clients for additional legal services.

    Lawyer has right to contact representatives of organizations interested in establishing a group or prepaid legal plan for members, beneficiaries, or third persons.

Sanctioned communications

Rule does *not prohibit* communications *authorized* by law or ordered by a court or tribunal [Rule 7.1(d)].

Prepaid and group legal services

Lawyer may participate in a prepaid or group legal services plan which uses personal solicitation if lawyer is not personally involved in solicitation, the organization is separate from the lawyer, and persons solicited are *not known* to need legal services [Rule 7.1(e)].

Coercive or unwanted communications

Even if an advertisement or solicitation would otherwise be allowed, the Rules are violated if the lawyer uses *coercion*, *duress*, or *harassment* or solicits a person who has *made known* that they do not want to be solicited.

Deleted Rules [Rule 7.4 and 7.5]

Rules 7.4 and 7.5 are deleted.

Political Contributions for Appointments [Rule 7.6]

Legal or judicial appointments

Lawyers or law firms shall not accept a government legal engagement or appointment by a judge if they *made or solicited political contributions* for legal engagement or appointment.

Notes for active learning

Chapter 9

Integrity of Profession

Bar Admissions and Disciplinary Matters [Rule 8.1]

Candor

Candidate for admission to the bar or a *lawyer subject to disciplinary action* shall not:

1) make a *false statement* of a *material fact* [Rule 8.1(a)] or

2) *fail to disclose* facts necessary to *correct a misapprehension* [Rule 8.1(b)].

Compliance

Lawyer must respond to lawful demands for information from admission or disciplinary authorities, except as protected by Rule 1.6.

Judicial and Legal Officers [Rule 8.2]

Disparaging comments

Lawyer shall not make *false or reckless statements* about the *qualifications or integrity* of a judge, magistrate, legal officer, or candidate for a judicial or legal office [Rule 8.2(a)].

Judicial conduct

Candidate for judicial office shall comply with the Code of Judicial Conduct [Rule 8.2(b)].

Reporting Professional Misconduct [Rule 8.3]

Affirmative duty for reporting

Lawyer who knows of another lawyer violating the Rules of Professional Conduct that raises a *substantial question* about that lawyer's *honesty or fitness* as a lawyer in other respects shall *inform the appropriate authority* [Rule 8.3(a)].

Judicial misconduct

Lawyer who knows that a judge has committed a *violation of judicial conduct* that raises a substantial question about the judge's fitness for office *shall inform* the appropriate authority [Rule 8.3(b)].

Exempt disclosures

Disclosure is not required for information protected by Rule 1.6 or gained by a lawyer or judge while participating in an approved lawyer's assistance program [Rule 8.3(c)].

Notes for active learning

Misconduct [Rule 8.4]

Acts of misconduct

Professional misconduct involves [Rule 8.4]:

> Violating the Rules of Professional Conduct or knowingly assisting or acting through another.

> commission of a criminal act reflecting adversely on lawyer's honesty or fitness as a lawyer.

> conduct involving dishonesty, fraud, or misrepresentation.

> conduct prejudicial to the administration of justice.

> implying an ability to improperly influence a government agency or official.

> assisting a judge or officer in violating applicable rules of conduct or law.

> engaging in conduct that adversely reflects fitness to practice law.

> engaging in harassment or discrimination related to the practice of law.

Representation and advocacy

Rule 8.4 does *not limit* a lawyer to *accept, decline*, or *withdraw representation* per Rule 1.16.

Rule 8.4 does *not preclude* legitimate advice or advocacy consistent with these Rules.

Professional responsibility vignette 13

During the last month, the following events occurred at the three-lawyer firm of which you are a partner.

Following a review of the firm's books, its outside accountant informed you and Abby that Paul had used funds kept in the firm's Clients' Trust Fund account ("Account") for personal purposes, with the result that the Account was depleted. On the same day, the firm received a demand from a client that the firm now delivers to him the net proceeds from a completed real estate transaction that had been held in the Account. There are insufficient funds in the Account to meet the client's demand.

Client's funds: lawyer shall promptly deliver funds when client is entitled to receive [Rule 1:15(b)].

Lawyer may withdraw from a client's fund account *only funds* belonging to *lawyer and not the client.*

Professional misconduct: a lawyer knowing that another lawyer has violated the Rules of Professional Conduct, which raises a *substantial question* about that lawyer's honesty, trustworthiness, or fitness, *shall inform* the appropriate authority [Rule 8.3].

It is professional misconduct for a lawyer to *engage in dishonesty* or *fraud* [Rule 8.4].

Paul has embezzled funds from the firm's trust fund account and has violated the disciplinary rule requiring that the client's funds be promptly delivered to the client.

He has also engaged in acts of fraud and dishonesty. Since you have unprivileged knowledge of this act, you must report his conduct to the appropriate authority.

Once you and Abby, as firm members, know that their trust fund account is underfunded, you and Abby should immediately restore the funds to the client's fund account, which Paul improperly withdrew.

You should comply with the disciplinary rule and pay the client promptly with funds you restored to the account.

You will have a cause of action to *recover funds from Paul*.

Professional responsibility vignette 14

Amy represented the Buyer in a suit for breach of contract by the Seller to sell a residential home to the Buyer. In conferences in preparation for the case, Buyer made the following requests to the lawyer: 1) in settlement negotiations with Seller's attorney, Amy should be sure to tell him, "We have evidence which documents the fact that he, Seller's attorney, commingled the real estate deposit with his funds,"2) Amy should make every effort possible to get an all-male jury because Seller is a woman.

2) Disciplinary charges: a lawyer is prohibited from threatening to present disciplinary charges solely to obtain an advantage in a private civil matter.

Lawyer should tell the buyer that they cannot honor the request to tell the seller's lawyer that the buyer has evidence that he commingled funds because that is a threat to present disciplinary charges to obtain an advantage in this case [Rule 8.4].

3) Manifesting bias: a lawyer is prohibited from appearing before a tribunal to engage in conduct manifesting bias on account of sex against any person.

While a lawyer has the right to peremptory challenges, systematically excluding females from the jury would manifest such a bias against women and probably violate this disciplinary rule.

The lawyer should *not acquiesce* to the client's request [Rule 8.4].

Discipline and Choice of Law [Rule 8.5]

Jurisdiction by license

If a lawyer is licensed in one jurisdiction, the Rules of Professional Conduct of that jurisdiction govern, even if occasionally, acting outside that jurisdiction.

Jurisdiction by continuous contact

If a lawyer practices continuously in a jurisdiction other than where licensed and the Rules of Professional Conduct differ, the *conflict of law principles* determines *applicable Rules*.

Lawyer may be *disciplined* in multiple jurisdictions for the *same conduct*.

Jurisdiction of federal courts

Lawyers who practice in federal tribunals are subject to rules of those tribunals even though they may conflict with the Rules of Professional Conduct of state licensing them.

Choice of law

Rules of professional conduct applied shall be *for conduct*:

> 1) in connection with a matter before a tribunal, rules of jurisdiction in which tribunal sits unless the tribunal provides otherwise; and

> 2) for other conduct, the rules of the jurisdiction in which the lawyer's *conduct occurred*, or, if the *predominant effect* of the conduct is in a different jurisdiction, rules of that jurisdiction shall be applied.

Lawyer shall *not be subject to discipline* if the lawyer's conduct conforms to the rules of a jurisdiction where the lawyer reasonably believes the predominant effect of the lawyer's conduct will occur.

Notes for active learning

Customer Satisfaction Guarantee

Your feedback is important because we strive to provide the highest quality prep materials. Email us comments or suggestions.

info@sterling–prep.com

We reply to emails – check your spam folder

Thank you for choosing our book!

Frank J. Addivinola, Ph.D., J.D., L.LM., MBA

The lead author and chief editor of this preparation guide is Dr. Frank Addivinola. With his outstanding education, professional training, legal and business experience, and university teaching, Dr. Addivinola lent his expertise to develop this book.

Attorney Frank Addivinola is admitted to practice law in several jurisdictions. He has served as an academic advisor and mentor for students and practitioners.

Dr. Addivinola earned his BA from Williams College, Master of Liberal Arts from Harvard University, Masters in Biotechnology at Johns Hopkins University, Masters of Science in Technology Management, and Masters of Business Administration at the University of Maryland, Juris Doctorate and Masters of Laws at Suffolk University, and Doctorate in Law and Public Policy at Northeastern University.

During his extensive teaching career, Professor Addivinola taught university courses in Introduction to Law and developed law course books. He received several awards for community service, research, and presentations.

Law Essentials series

Constitutional Law	Criminal Law and Criminal Procedure
Contracts	Business Associations
Evidence	Conflict of Laws
Real Property	Family Law
Torts	Secured Transactions
Civil Procedure	Trusts and Estates

Visit our Amazon store

Bar Exam Preparation Guides

Comprehensive Glossary of Legal Terms

Over 2,100 essential legal terms defined and explained. An excellent reference source for law students, practitioners, and readers seeking an understanding of legal vocabulary and applications.

Visit our Amazon store

Made in the USA
Las Vegas, NV
20 March 2024

87462026R00090